My Lover, My Friend

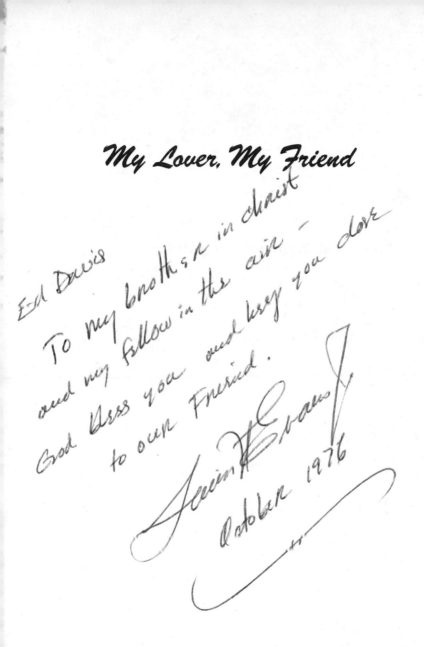

Ed Davis

To my brother in christ
and my fellow in the air —
God bless you and keep you dear
to our Friend.

Louis H Evans Jr

October 1976

BY COLLEEN TOWNSEND EVANS

A New Joy
Love Is an Everyday Thing

BY COLLEEN AND LOUIS H. EVANS, JR.

My Lover, My Friend

My Lover, My Friend

Colleen Townsend Evans
and
Louis H. Evans Jr.

Fleming H. Revell Company
Old Tappan, New Jersey

Scripture quotations identified RSV are from the Revised Standard Version of the Bible, copyrighted 1946, 1952, © 1971 and 1973.

The poem by David W. Augsburger appears on page 1 of *The Love-Fight* (Scottdale, Pa.: Herald Press, 1973). Used by permission of Herald Press.

The poem *Lord, Could You Make It a Little Better?* by Robert A. Raines is used by permission of Word Books, Publisher, Waco, Texas.

Library of Congress Cataloging in Publication Data

Evans, Colleen Townsend.
   My lover, my friend.

1. Marriage. 2. Christian life—Presbyterian authors. I. Evans, Louis Hadley, date, joint author. II. Title.
HQ734.E87   261.8′34′2   76–22480
ISBN 0–8007–0751–6

FOR

Dan, Tim, Andie, Jamie,
who have brought so much joy
into our marriage simply by
being uniquely themselves

Contents

Gratefully . . .

THROUGH THE YEARS there have been so many people who have touched our lives and influenced our thinking, and we would like to give them all credit for anything of value we have borrowed, made part of our lives, and now share here. But—our "rememberers" aren't that good! So, to those who have lectured at conferences we have attended, written books we have read, and whose ideas we have absorbed to the point where we don't know where theirs stop and ours begin —*thank you!*

There is one person whose book we have read not once, but many times, and we want to take this opportunity to thank Dr. David R. Mace for all *Whom God Hath Joined* has meant to us.

We also are very grateful to our friends who have shared both the joys and honest struggles of their marriages. They have added so much to our lives and to the writing of this book.

Our thanks, too, to some special people who have exercised their gift of helps and given us the practical

9

aid we needed to see this project through to fruition: Jayne Crawford for her typing and Jeanine and Gene Arnold for a quiet, loving atmosphere in which to work.

COLLEEN AND LOUIS H. EVANS, JR.
WASHINGTON, D.C.

There's Hope For a Great Institution

THE TRAIN FOR New York was filling up fast. I found an empty seat beside a young woman—she was in her late twenties, attractive and well dressed. We began to talk, sharing our mutual sorrow over the dumping grounds of America as our train rolled past acres of junked cars, city trash heaps, and strewn backyards. We found we had similar concerns in a number of areas. As the miles clickety-clacked away and our conversation continued, I found the young woman to be surprisingly open about her personal life, specifically her relationship with her boyfriend. He wanted her to live with him, but she wasn't sure she would and she wasn't sure she wouldn't. "I'm definitely not ready for marriage," she said emphatically, "and maybe I never will be."

"What do you feel about marriage?" I asked.

"What do *you* feel about it?" she asked, pointing to my wedding ring.

"I'm sold on it," I answered. "But, as with any rela-

11

tionship worth its salt, it has to be worked at. Good marriages don't just happen—and even the best marriages have problems that need to be worked out."

"Why stick with it, then?" she asked, looking somewhat pensively at a fold she was adjusting in her skirt. I had a feeling we had touched a sensitive point. "If there is *any* kind of hassle or inconvenience in a relationship, why stick around?"

I shared with her for a while the deep satisfaction of a committed relationship as opposed to the popular trend of "punching out" when things get tense. I tried to be honest about some of the hang-ups I had brought into my marriage, about the mixture of love and honesty from my wife, Colleen, that I felt characterized the covenant we have together. I explained how Christ had been a great Therapist in our relationship, stripping back the layers of pride I had carefully maintained and adding new styles of openness in which I could communicate my need instead of continuing in my old patterns of self-sufficiency. I told her how Christ had given Colleen, who was raised in a home without a father, the strength and security she needed to emerge as a whole person. I said we felt it took two people, secure enough to risk growing and changing together, to make a good marriage. I talked a bit about our kids —about the terrific joy they had brought into our lives and about some of the honest encounters we had had with them. I guess I got pretty excited, because she looked straight at me and smiled. "You're *really* turned on by marriage, aren't you?" she said.

"Does it show?" I laughed.

"Sure does, but I like it. You really find it fulfilling?"

"Tremendously!"

"Well, you're one of the few persons I've met who feels that way. You give me hope—but it sure has to work against a lot of bad publicity." Then she told me about her folks' divorce, which had been a source of great pain in her life. She also had a number of friends who had tried marriage and were opting out.

"Not very good data, is it?" I queried.

"Nope, but I sure wish it was."

The train began to slow down. We were coming to her station. She stood up and took her bag from the rack above. Then, with a warm yet wistful look, she tossed me a parting word. "Take care of the good thing you've got going."

I fumbled for a card in my wallet and handed it to her. A smile crossed her face. "A preacher. . . . Wouldn't you know!" she quipped.

"But marriage is not just for preachers," I got out just before she was beyond earshot.

I think I understand what had soured that young woman on marriage. She was like so many other young people I had counseled. They were painfully disappointed with family life as they had known it. They wanted no part of the Standard American Package—the money, the big cars, the house with the oversized mortgage, the pressures, and finally the legal hassles of divorce. I imagine my young friend had been given "everything"—except the time, attention, and affection of her parents. Now she was saying, *"This* is marriage? Not for me!"

But I felt I heard her saying something more: "I wish it were different. I'd like to believe in marriage, but I just can't believe in the ones I've seen."

The train jolted forward and we were on our way once again. Alone with my thoughts, I found myself wondering—yet again—what goes wrong with so many marriages.

Is she, and the many others who share her feelings, being "turned off" by marriages that have given in to the ease of a convenience society, the escape exits of contract relationships, and the staggering changes that are molding our society by sheer pressure?

"Convenience" has become a key word in our culture. And thank God for many of the conveniences: automobiles, gas stoves, electric refrigerators, airplanes, and what have you. But tragically, convenience has also become a hallmark of our relationships, and there's the rub! "I'll stand by you—so long as it is convenient. But if things get tough, don't expect me to stay around. You're gentle on my mind." That kind of attitude is devastating to the human personality. If a child feels a parent will opt out of the relationship as soon as things become inconvenient, his very foundations are shaken. Each of us longs to be important to somebody —to somebody who will brave all sorts of barriers to come to us in our moment of need, pushing aside the inconvenience. Each of us needs someone who will be available. Commitment says, "I'll be with you through thick and thin!" That is security!

Sometimes both partners to the marriage contract are aware of the "small print," but often only one party knows what it says. Suddenly that partner makes the simple accusation, "You have broken the contract." And the relationship comes to a sudden end.

"But I didn't know," comes the anguished cry of the other, who did not know the conditions of the contract, which were: "You be the successful provider, and I will love you always. But fail, and it is all over." Or perhaps it was: "Be the beautiful, healthy entertainer for my business contacts, and I will forever take good care of your needs. But once you show dissatisfaction with the meaningless chatter of cocktail parties—or if you become ill and unable to function as a hostess—we're finished."

A covenant, on the other hand, says "My commitment is to you as a person, not to the roles you fulfill for my satisfaction. There is nothing you can say or do that will make me stop loving you."

The basis for this covenant comes from God himself, who does not turn away from us, his children, just because we have done wrong. He comes back to us again and again, often with honest encounter, but always with untiring love. As I see it, the great example of this love is Jesus, who was God's act of love toward a hostile world. Nothing could drive God from his covenant: his commitment was firm. No degree of inconvenience and no broken agreements could supress the flow of his love.

All of us yearn for this kind of commitment from the one *most* important to us. Without it, we just never become the people we were meant to be. Without commitment, we also exhibit an interesting psychological response. Wanting something so basic—yet being frustrated in finding it—we begin to fear the very thing we long for, or we try to rationalize it away. Perhaps this is why some people are turning away from the covenant of marriage to new philosophies of "contract" marriages and convenience relationships. We believe this is part of the problem. Add to this the massive changes in our society in recent years—our technological liberation, the population explosion, the Women's Movement, and so on—plus the lack of authentic, attractive models for marriage, and it's no wonder my young friend was confused and turned off by the institution of marriage.

And yet the search goes on. According to a National Institute of Mental Health survey, 87 percent of the college students polled listed family life as one of their most important goals. It seems it isn't marriage as a relationship that is in question but the *quality* of the marriage relationship. People are hungry for more fulfilling, deeper relationships in marriage. They are beginning to define marriage as two people who love and like each other, who can have fun together, who can share life's highest goals, and who can consciously make a lifelong commitment to each other and to each other's growth as a person. A new generation—and many of the older generation as well—want something *more* than an empty traditional definition of marriage.

And that is the purpose of this book—to supply that "more" quality.

Colleen and I feel there *is* more. Marriage has a thrilling potential that can be realized by those who are willing to stretch and grow through their commitment to each other and through the process of openness and honesty in their life together. There is much of the old that is worth rediscovering, although admittedly some of the traditional must be challenged. All around us are new discoveries waiting to be incorporated into marriage to make it a richer experience.

We'll be very straightforward; this is a book of *hope!* Hope, yes—but not a book pushing a neat little formula that will work in some magical way for every marriage. No two people are alike—no two marriages are alike— God's creation is full of exciting diversity, especially when it comes to people. Within his creative guidelines, there is room for this diversity; he honors it, and so do we. So there will be no surefire answers for all the couples of the world, no "pink pill" approach to successful marriage. Rather, we would like to look with you at some biblical premises in light of our contemporary scene. What, for instance, is the nature of authority and the meaning of submission? We intend t dig deeply into the liberating love of Jesus Christ, the Designer of marriage, as we come to grips with some of the problems every marriage has to face. We want to consider the exciting interdependence of persons and the roles of husband and wife not as they are predetermined solely by sex or tradition but as they are seen through the New Testament prism of the gifts of the Spirit. We want to look at seven basics of a good marriage. We also want to share some steps in the sometimes painful yet liberating process of communication.

Enough of what we want to write about—and just a word about *how* we will be writing it. At first we considered doing this book as a dialogue, but we found that to be a very difficult form for us. We then moved on to the idea of a monologue—two persons' ideas presented as one voice—but that was both contrived and awkward. Finally, with the help of a few close friends, we decided that the most natural way would be for each of us to write certain chapters, choosing the areas for which our individual gifts equip us and where we feel most at home.

One more thing—we have no illusions about our ability to do justice to this vast subject of marriage. We already feel the frustration of not being able to deal with certain areas in depth—and we are keenly aware of the many aspects of life together we are leaving completely untouched, either because of our own limitations or the limitations of time and space. However, our prayer is that in the simplicity of what is shared here, there will be a ministry to some. For we see marriage as the most exciting and fulfilling of all human relationships. It is the most practical arena of self-discovery, the most basic building block of any society. It is more than a loving, supportive relationship. Marriage brings together two human beings with everything that is theirs. It invites them to contribute whatever they are—and *all* that they are—to a new style of life. Marriage enables a man and a woman to give each other the gift of themselves in a lifelong commitment. It is the place of intimate discovery and sharing in which two people can say, "My lover—my friend."

This is my lover,
This is my friend....

Song of Solomon 5:16

1

He Makes It Possible

ANYONE WHO REALLY knows me knows how deeply I feel about marriage. I'm a believer . . . I think it's great! But marriage, no matter how good, is not the answer to life. God is. I really believe it is in knowing him that we are able to know marriage and all the meaningful relationships of life as he meant them to be. Even the *capacity* to love is his gift—a gift given so that we might choose to love him and one another. But his giving is not limited to that initial gift of love—all through marriage he continues to supply the resources we need for a deep, satisfying life together by the ongoing work of his Spirit in our lives.

We read that as God went about the work of creation, he looked around and saw that everything was good—except for one thing: "It is not good for man to be alone." And so we were created, male and female, for many purposes, of course, but primarily for the high purpose of companionship. What a great and wonderful thing that God did! And yet (I must remind myself) it is not the gift, but the Giver who has priority in my life.

So often we expect a husband or a wife to be in our life
what only God can be, and the burden is too great. A
good friend of ours who has just gone through a painful
break with his wife keeps saying: "She expected me to
be everything to her, and there just wasn't *enough* of
me to meet her needs." The number one spot in every
heart is meant for God, and things just don't function
well when we insist on putting someone else in a place
reserved only for him. Rather, there is deep truth in the
concept that until we love God more than our husband
or wife, we will never know how freely and deeply we
can love the one with whom we have made a life covenant. To love is to yield to another's love. When the love
of God in Christ invades us, we are able to take his gift
of love and love our mate—and others—in a way surprising even to ourselves.

When God comes first in a marriage, something happens for which I personally am very grateful. I know
there is something more than my relationship with
Louie on which I can depend. As important as my marriage is to me, I need to know it doesn't stand on its
own. Our individual relationships with Christ give it a
basis of support. I suppose the explanation lies in the
fact that our marriage doesn't have to carry all its own
weight, that we are not a closed system without any
help from the outside. So many couples seem to live
only for each other, and when something threatens
their relationship, there is no one to come to their res-
cue. How much more helpful it is when differences

and problems arise, for two people to go to Christ. As they come closer to him, their reference point, they will find themselves closer to one another. I know. We've been there, and it works. It isn't that I always have to accept Louie's position, or that he has to bow to mine. When we both seek God in a situation, there is often a third, more creative, answer to the difference we share. The bonus is that as two people *both* submit to Christ—and to one another out of reverence for him —there is something above and beyond that guarantees their love for each other. This is the best security base I know for any marriage—not our outer circumstances or our theology of marriage—but our relationships with him! *Christ* is our security. He is also our great "constant" in life.

Today, as I was standing at the washing machine, stuffing it with dirty clothes, I realized that just a few days earlier I had been standing in the same spot doing the same thing—but my feelings were at an entirely different place. I had been strangely discouraged—I can't remember why—it doesn't matter. The point is, my *feelings* were undependable. At that earlier moment I was so lacking in confidence I could not imagine how Louie could possibly have been so dumb as to choose me for his wife. Silly, perhaps, but that is what my feelings told me. I remember sighing and thinking, "Well, Lord, you're in charge around here. . . . I'm tired [which, come to think of it, may have been my problem] so please take over my feelings, because I know these aren't of you!"

Well, today it was a different story. I was rested, my feelings were behaving, and I even wondered if Louie knew how lucky he was to have me for his wife. In fact I could hardly wait for him to come home so that I could ask him.

Our feelings vary from day to day. A very close friend who has one of the greatest marriages I know shared with me a feeling she had very early in their married life. One day, all of a sudden, she looked at her husband and her heart sank. Something had happened to her feelings for him. The thrill was gone. She was conscious of saying to herself, "Okay, this is it. This is the way it's going to be. I've made a commitment to God—and to my husband—and I'm going to live by that commitment, not my feelings." And so she proceeded by faith to love her husband, sincerely if not with the same sense of thrill and depth of emotional feeling. It wasn't long before one day, just as suddenly as the feeling had gone, the feeling returned . . . and more! It overflowed!

In the years that have followed, her feelings have known the ebb and flow—the highs and the lows—of a creative personal life. But her love—their love—has grown steadily, and their marriage has been a *joy*, not only for them but for anyone who knows them well. She learned a great lesson—that just as we can't live the Christian life according to our feelings all the time, neither can we judge our marriage by a feeling of the moment. God is a great stabilizer, a great constant in our lives—and in our life together.

He is also the Great Therapist for a husband and wife. We all come into marriage with hang-ups . . . mistaken ideas, the myth of perfection; and the need to grow. We have to resist the urge to remold our mate, and we must open ourselves instead to the work of God in our own life. Therapy begins the moment we honestly pray, "Make me the person I should be in my marriage." When I think of all the areas of my life God has had to work on since I first prayed that prayer, I am amazed at his patience and faithfulness. Beginning with the basic security I needed to be able to give myself away in a lifelong covenant, God has again and again provided all the resources I needed for emotional growth and freedom. And the work goes on . . . there isn't a day in my life when I don't need my "Liberator-Therapist."

God is also the Great Provider of our physical needs. When God takes care of us, we are getting some of the best possible direction on priorities and finances. I remember feeling such confidence during the early part of our marriage when we were in seminary. We were always short of money, yet we were certain that God would provide what we actually needed. And he did! There was a time when we were out of money for two weeks. We had eaten everything in the cupboard, and I had given Louie the last of our food for lunch: a hard-boiled egg and a glass of tomato juice. Poor Louie started mumbling about taking me away from a career with a good income only to drag me off to seminary and starvation. We laugh about it now, but Louie says at the time he felt painfully inadequate. I remember how we knelt in the tiny living room of our basement apartment and prayed for resources. Later in the day Louie took a break from his studies to check the mail and found a letter from a church where he had preached six weeks earlier. He had not expected any payment from it, but there it was, forty dollars! And more! It was a sign from the Lord that he would provide—and he always has. Things have been tight much of the time, but there has always been enough for the important things . . . the right things . . . and enough to share with others.

There have been a few times when our eyes have been too big for our pocketbooks, and God has always drawn us back to the simpler life that is what seems to be right for us. I think of the house we bought some years ago. It was a nice house with a lovely, big yard and a gorgeous view of the ocean. It was a bit too much for us to handle, perhaps, but oh, so pretty. It took only a few months for that "too much" to pull us under financially, and we couldn't wait to sell it and get back to the simple life. The little house that took its place was beautiful beyond words—because it was not "too much." It was right.

Another great thing Christ does in a marriage is to forgive and heal. A marriage is closer to being genuinely Christian at its core not when it is free of all difficulties but when both partners are open to the work of God in their lives. There is no perfect marriage, no marriage that does not need God's forgiving ways as part of its everyday life-style. In this atmosphere two people can feel forgiven by God and so be generous in forgiving one another. In this atmosphere healing takes place, and love and growth walk hand in hand. It is a beautiful thing to see a couple allow God to release his grace and power in their lives at the very point of their need.

I know I'm a hopeless idealist, but I strongly feel there is no relationship too far gone for Christ to make it new. He can heal any hurt, restore lost hope, renew love. But, of course, there is a condition—it requires *two* willing people to make the miracle work.

Amy and Peter were marvelous people. Both of them were intelligent, attractive, warm human beings. They had been married for over twenty years, had four lively children, and from the outside things looked great. But on the inside their life together had turned sour. They both worked at consuming jobs, had little time for each other, and when they were together they began to feel like strangers. With *their* communication system out, they began to be drawn to other people. At first, it was just someone to talk to over lunch, someone to listen. But as their needs grew, the "only a friend" plot thickened, and the time came when they had to face the fact that they were in trouble. You've heard lots of stories like it, and they usually end up in the divorce court. But in this case that was not the end. In a real sense it was only the beginning . . . because Amy and Peter had all the makings for a miracle. They basically loved God, and down deep they wanted their marriage to work, so they were open to help. They sought a counselor who shared their faith, and he took them through a long and painful journey of discovery and insight. He finally urged them to take the hurts—and all that needed forgiving—to Christ, the only one who can really handle such things. I know they were frightened at this point. I still remember the tremble in Amy's voice when she asked me to pray for them as they took that step together by faith. What if it didn't work? But as they yielded themselves to Christ for his forgiveness and healing, the miracle of Christian marriage happened, as it will when two people seek the mind of Christ. There were forgiveness and healing—and such a new love was born in their hearts in the months that followed that they felt they wanted to be remarried.

Because they had never divorced, that couldn't be, but with their minister they designed a simple, beautiful service of reuniting. On a lovely Sunday afternoon their children stood up with them as they rededicated their lives to Christ—and to each other. I was lucky enough to be there that day and, believe me, there wasn't a dry eye in the church. Your marriage may not need the major reuniting my friends needed, but every marriage needs reuniting in some way every day.

And every marriage needs healing—for there is no way to love and share life's *most* intimate relationship without being hurt.

A scene that took place years ago crosses my mind and becomes part of my life again, as I think of the need for healing in marriage. Hazel, a beautiful woman in her late twenties, was standing at our door saying good-night after a meeting in our home. A gentle breeze blowing through the open door brought the scents of summer (gardenia and jasmine) to us, and as we stood laughing and talking, the light from the lamp on the porch caught Hazel in its aura. I remember thinking how attractive she was—inside and out—and then the next thought followed predictably: "a good catch for some fortunate man."

At that moment our youngest son—who had apparently heard us and climbed out of his crib to join the fun—toddled up to me and nuzzled his head against my body lovingly. I picked him up and balanced him on one hip while his body curled naturally against mine. I continued talking to Hazel until I noticed tears in her eyes. She was staring at Jamie and said, after what seemed like a very long time, "It must be wonderful to have a family!"

"Oh, it is," I replied. "Hectic sometimes, but wonderful. But you'll know that for yourself one day—that is, I'd be surprised if *you didn't!*"

At that, fear crossed her face and she said, "No . . . *never.* I'll never get married—never have a family. I couldn't take the pain that comes with loving that much." With that she turned abruptly and walked out of the light into the darkness of the street.

"Hazel, you're right," I thought. "Love, and your heart will be broken—not once, but many times. Pain is an inherent part of love. But Hazel, you're also wrong, for you've failed to remember that God is a Healer. He promises to be part of the covenant relationship you make when you marry. Because love is tender, you *will* hurt and be hurt. There *will* be pain. But he will be there to heal the hurt and to set you on your way stronger than before. Say *no* to love and you are saying *no* to life. Rather—trust God, and live. For he is the Great Healer—the Great Forgiver—in things both great and small."

I agree with Lloyd Ogilvie when he says, "We are far too timid in sharing the secret of Christian marriage. It is a Christ-healed, spirit-filled relationship" (from material presented at Continental Congress on the Family, St. Louis, 1975).

He is the one who provides love, security, patience, stability, forgiveness, healing—those things we need for a great marriage, not because we are unusual people but because he is a great God. As husbands and wives we were never meant to go it alone. He makes it all possible.

2

Who's in Charge Here?

THERE IS A LOT of pain in many marriages—much of it rooted in the problem of authority.

Kirk was a strong individual, highly creative and well known in business circles. His wife, Carolyn, was a gifted person, energetic, efficient, imaginative, and one to throw herself with all her might into anything she did. But she didn't have much opportunity to exercise her strengths. To say that Kirk was difficult to live with would be an understatement. He was bossy, demanding, not always ethical, and often insensitive to other people's feelings—especially to Carolyn's. He took it for granted that she would go along with him without question.

Some years ago Carolyn told me she had to make a decision. She had tried to have an honest, open discussion with her husband, but he couldn't handle it. He interpreted her concern over his behavior as criticism and went into a rage. It was her complete approval and absolute acquiescence he demanded, nothing less. So Carolyn had to decide between ending the marriage by exercising her strengths—or yielding in every way to her husband. She chose to yield.

Carolyn realized she had a limited number of choices. She could go through the war of separation and divorce—and war it would be—leaving emotional, financial, and spiritual devastation in its wake. Or she could submit to Kirk's pathologies, learning to deal with his tirades and self-centeredness, and hoping that some day Kirk might change.

In choosing to submit to her partner she was giving up the ideal of an open, honest, and shared life. Instead, she would have to bite her tongue, swallow her pride, and put a lot of her creative abilities into cold storage. But that was the only way she saw of saving their marriage. Carolyn had bought a kind of "peace."

Some forms of peace are not as creative as others. In Carolyn's case it meant the loss of some outstanding human potential; and yet all was not lost. Some of the time Kirk was a delight—alive, interesting, jovial, even thoughtful, and certainly never a bore! There were compensations, and Carolyn chose to live with them. It was her choice, and I won't fault her for that!

Carolyn's decision was not without its costs. Part of the strain she bore was evident in painful migraines. As years went on, her three children—fine people—carried scars that caused serious trouble. That was a big price to pay for "peace."

If Carolyn had chosen the first alternative, that of divorce, she would have refused to submit, and there would have been a rupture in the relationship. Perhaps the cause would have been tagged "immaturity," "an inability to deal with frustration," a "lack of communications skills and ways of dealing with anger," or maybe it would have been described as an escape from a demeaning, destructive partnership. Whatever the label, the experience would have been painful.

The second alternative meant submitting to another's weakness and living with pain—but keeping the marriage together. In making her choice Carolyn followed what she felt was the biblical view of submitting to one's husband in all circumstances. Hadn't Paul said, "Wives, be subject to your husbands, as to the Lord. For the husband is the head of the wife as Christ is the head of the church. . . . As the church is subject to Christ, so let wives also be subject in everything to their husbands" (Ephesians 5:22–24 RSV)? Peter said the same thing: "Likewise you wives, be submissive to your husbands, so that some, though they do not obey the word, may be won without a word by the behavior of their wives . . ." (1 Peter 3:1 RSV).

The Pharisees of Jesus' day would have agreed with Carolyn. They took God's curse on woman seriously: "To the woman he said, 'I will greatly multiply your pain in childbearing; in pain you shall bring forth children, yet your desire shall be for your husband, and he shall rule over you'" (Genesis 3:16 RSV).

In the Jewish culture of the New Testament a woman was definitely a second-rate citizen. Sons inherited

land, but daughters received only maintenance. If a
wife found anything, it belonged to her husband, as did
the work of her hands. Even a woman's inheritance,
should there be no male to receive it, could be used by
her husband for his desires. A woman was not given a
teaching position among the laity in the synagogue—if
she had a question, she could ask her husband when
they got home. The cultural conditioning was so deep
it is not surprising that it found expression in the teaching of the New Testament writers themselves.

But let us take a second look at the biblical material.
It appears there are four phases to humanity in Christ:
(1) created innocence, (2) the Fall, (3) re-creation in
Christ, and (4) glorification. I will not get into the last,
except to say that any Christian who is aware of the
promise of Christ and believes it, looks forward to that
day of Christ's triumphal return. At this point, however, I want only to look at the first three phases.

The first was the state of innocence in which man and
woman were created with a kind of parity. God created
mankind male and female. "And God blessed *them,*
and God said to *them,* 'Be fruitful and multiply, and fill
the earth and subdue it'. . ." (Genesis 1:28 RSV, italics
mine). Evidently the potential for dominion was given
to both male and female. When God created woman,
he created her as helper (in the Hebrew, *azar*) to man.
But this word *azar* does not imply inferiority or second-
rate status. God himself is *azar* to man, "A very present
help in time of need." If anything, the word indicates

man's incompleteness without woman—his need for her, even as man is incomplete without a relationship with God. Likewise, woman needs man. So close is the need factor that when man was presented with woman, he cried out, "Bone of my bone, and flesh of my flesh!" His very joy was an expression of his need for her. In this phase of humanity, male and female became one flesh. The two were one. They shared a unity of need and complementation.

In the second phase of humanity, that of the Fall, all of life came under the curse of sin. The relationship of man and woman was affected in that man became the ruler of woman, and the wife from that time on was subject to the authority of her husband. The earth was subject to the futility of mankind's distorted dominion, and man himself was cursed to wrest his living from a thistle-filled and thorn-bearing earth. We must remember that all the Old Testament was written during this phase of the Fall and the curse. It was during this phase that Pharisaism was born and developed, with all its legal rules and burdens that Christ described as "heavy burdens placed on people's backs which [the Pharisees] would not lift a finger to lighten" (*see* Matthew 23:4). Christ was angered by the insensitivity and judgmentalism that pointed a finger at outward behavior without attempting to understand the inward need of the individual. It was that burdensome legalism that drew Paul's sharpest criticism—that the law could not give life or liberate souls oppressed by the curse.

Thank God, we are not stuck in the mire of this second phase. In Christ we have moved on to the third phase of humanity. Through his death and victorious Resurrection we have been set free from the curse. In him we are made new creatures! Here, in this third phase, the image of God's original design is replacing the old forms of legalism and subjugation. "The old has passed away and the new is in the process of becoming!" (*See* 2 Corinthians 5:17.) Old inferiorities are eliminated; woman has become again the "helper," the peer of man. ". . . there is neither male nor female; for you are all one in Christ Jesus. And if you are Christ's, then you are Abraham's offspring, heirs according to promise" (Galatians 3:28, 29 RSV). Former lords have become servants after the example of Christ striving to bring everyone to maturity in Christ (*see* Colossians 1:28). Husbands now are to give up their lives for their wives as Christ gave up his life for the church, that they might be presented before him "in splendor," the splendor of their full maturity. The subjugations once operating under the law are now removed. Man's subjugation to the law, woman's subjugation to man, mankind's subjugation to death, are now replaced by all of mankind's subjugation to Jesus Christ. Every man, woman, and youth has direct access to Jesus Christ through the Holy Spirit. And through the same Spirit, Jesus Christ has access to the mind and will of every man, woman, and youth. Therefore, if anyone puts any other relationship ahead of that to Jesus Christ, he or she is not worthy of Christ (*see* Matthew 10:34–39).

Instead of lordships that hold others in inferior positions, those who have experienced Christ's redemption are called to a life of service. Now, as Christians, we submit to one another out of reverence for Christ, out of reverence for his example of servanthood, out of reverence for his liberating death and Resurrection, out of reverence for the gifts that his Holy Spirit creates in each believer.

The Christian wife submits herself to her husband—of course! My wife submits to me in a hundred different ways! But that is not all. I also submit to her. The Spirit calls us to a mutual submission. "Be subject to *one another* out of reverence for Christ" (Ephesians 5:21 RSV) is the key verse here (my italics), and *mutual submission* is the overall theme of the verses that follow. A wife is to submit to her husband "as to the Lord" (Ephesians 5:22 RSV)—but that does not mean that her husband *is* her lord. She is to serve her husband in the line of serving Christ. (The Greek word meaning "as" indicates intention, the intention of a wife to serve her husband as he attempts to achieve his dominion over some part of God's creation—just as she serves Christ and the realization of his kingdom.)

Compare Ephesians 5:22 with its parallel passage, Colossians 3:18 RSV: "Wives, be subject to your husbands, as is fitting [proper] in the Lord." This means to us that wives are to please the Lord primarily—and then they are to submit to their husbands as the husbands labor for the Lord's kingdom. A Christian wife will submit whatever resources she has to undergird her husband in his efforts to complete Christ's ministry. She will go with him where he feels God is leading him to work, because he is probably the chief breadwinner. She submits to the valid demands made upon her because of the scheduling involved in his work; she makes the way straight for his endeavors. She is indeed his "helper," someone he needs for his completion, just as he needs the Lord and his resources.

If, however, the husband demands something that is outside the will of Christ and requires the wife to give up those things that belong to Christ or to others, then his wife is under no obligation to obey her husband if in so doing she must disobey Christ, her Lord. Any husband who makes such demands on his wife simply demonstrates his foolishness and misplaced ego.

Some Christian teachers insist that a woman should go along with *anything* her husband asks because he is her "lord." After listening to some of the things such husbands demand of their wives—whether in scheduling priorities or in sexual activities—I am convinced that a wife only reinforces her husband's arrogance and demeans herself by submitting to him. Nobody wins by such appeasement. The wife who goes along with a husband's desire when she feels it is contrary to Christ denies her Lord and permits her husband to stumble headlong into a pit of error.

We understand that many wives during the Watergate debacle were in the dark as to their husbands' activities. But one wife, discovering what her husband was involved in, blew the whistle by calling upon him to act in a moral way. He did! He withdrew from the questionable activities and was not caught in the whirlpool of misdeeds.

I know that if I am bound on a course that Colleen feels will be less than God's best, I am going to hear about it. And I love her for that. If she were to submit to me in such a way as to lessen her clarity of commitment to Christ, I would be very unhappy, because I deeply believe that God's will is the best thing that can happen to us. Often my wife is the instrument of challenge through which I become aware of God's will for my life. I am grateful, even though it may, and sometimes does, sting my male pride. We have seen more marriages blessed because a woman "by her chaste and reverent behavior" was not only loyal to her husband in chastity, but reverent to Christ in obedience, than by a woman covering her Christian witness and denying her Lord.

When the question comes up, "Who's in charge here?" the Christian wife should be able to say, clearly and boldly, "Jesus Christ."

A few years ago, when I was considering a call to another church, Colleen exercised a strong influence on my decision. She confronted me, mildly but firmly, because she thought I was not open to the new situation. (I wasn't. I had five good reasons why I shouldn't go!) Finally she said, "Honey, I just don't think you're open-minded about the matter!"

At first I smarted under the confrontation, but she jarred me loose from a "dead center" position. We agreed that I should go away for a few days and pray the thing through. On my return I was "in neutral gear," willing to go or willing to stay. In this attitude we went to the new city, preaching in a nearby church, and met with the committee for a long afternoon of openness and candor that I doubt would have been possible if I either had desperately wanted the position or had been close-minded about it. We put all our cards on the table, as honestly as we could. When the call came, *I* accepted it. It was *my* decision. And yet *we* accepted it. It was my decision and I knew Colleen would go along with whatever I decided, once I gave open consideration to it. But we talked and prayed it over so thoroughly that our minds had a common response when the voice on the other end of the phone said, "It is the unanimous decision of the committee . . ." and so on, and so on. I felt good about letting my wife influence my life. Her sensitivity, her gift of discernment, were much-needed elements. If I had been hard-headed about it, I could have denied her challenge and missed God's direction. In that case, there would have been grave doubts about the quality of my leadership. Jesus Christ is her lord, not I, and when she submits to his lordship, I am blessed.

Yes, husbands also submit to their wives, loving them

"as Christ loved the church and gave himself up for her, that he might sanctify her . . ." (Ephesians 5:25, 26 RSV). To me this passage means that Christ loves the church, that he wants her to be all that she can be, and that he gives himself to the church, to bring her to her full potential as God designed her, in the splendor of her maturity, cleansed of anything that would hold her back from the full realization of God's design. In doing this Christ is definitely in charge; there was no doubt about his lordship. But his style of lordship turns authority right side up for the first time in history. He becomes a servant-lord. I believe this to be the model for the Christian husband.

David and Nancy Low are one of the exciting young couples we have met since coming to Washington. He is a financial lawyer, and she is a top-flight public relations administrator. Only recently have they come to Washington, and the reason for their coming is a good illustration of a servant-head of a home.

After working in another state for a well-known and respected political leader, Nancy was offered a very high position in a federal government agency. This opportunity was made even more exciting by the fact that it had never before been offered to a woman. David felt the offer was a high honor and urged Nancy to accept it. He was confident he could find a job in his field in Washington. So, submitting to Nancy's career potential, they pulled up stakes and settled here.

Some men would be threatened by this type of situation. If a man wanted to prove that he didn't need other people, if he were an emotional do-it-yourselfer, then he might resist the emergence of his wife's career, especially if it was an outstanding one. But David is a strong man, eager and able to become a servant to Nancy's development. That is healthy "headship" and management.

Modern corporate management has taken a page right out of our book and handed it back to the Christian home. Douglas McGregor, in *The Human Side of Enterprise,* speaks of x-style and y-style managers. The x-style managers are the authoritarian decision makers who hand down their executive memos each morning and watch their "good" vice presidents doing exactly what they are told. These managers have greatly restricted their enterprises to the limits of their own creative abilities and mistakes. They leave little room for the growth and development of others unless that growth happens to coincide with the interests of the "big shot." So much potential goes to waste in corporations under this sort of management that it is no wonder morale is often low. People don't like to be kept down or left out of decision making that affects them.

The y-style managers, on the other hand, guarantee a process in which others can develop under their leadership. They watch for others' strengths with which to meet the various corporate needs, provide the resources for their development, and give over responsibility while keeping communication close. No wonder morale is high in corporations where persons are encouraged to grow to their full potential!

Why not apply this concept to the home? Notice how Christ delegates authority when he mandates various functions to his disciples. All these functions have to do with liberation and development, not subjugation.

I believe the husband *is* the head of the house. The question for me is not "Who's in charge here?" but rather, "What sort of leadership is being exercised?" There are *x*-style and *y*-style husbands. Colleen and I are deeply concerned about the heavy emphasis on *x*-style husbands in many manuals on the Christian home. Instead of calling forth the abilities of others, these husbands act like little generals ordering their troops around and demanding submission on all points. Or they gallantly try to be "the fearless leader" in *all* aspects of their homes, even in areas where they are not gifted. In living out the *x*-style they deny the servant role and fail to resource others to their development in the home. Everybody feels their awkwardness and embarrassment. Heavy burdens, indeed!

It works best when the husband uses his authority to create an atmosphere in which the potentials of each member of the family are identified and stimulated and nurtured.

I love flying! And I have had both styles of instructors. The *x*-style often used a lot of four-letter words to impress their students with their toughness, and usually they had a superior attitude. I remember one who got into the plane and said nothing. There I was, waiting for some indication of what the lesson of the day would be and—nothing but silence. Finally the instructor grumped, "Well, you want to fly or not? What are you waiting for?" Then, without giving me a moment to reply, he blurted out, "Ever heard of ground effect?"

I hesitated for a moment and was just about to explain what I knew when he sarcastically retorted, "I didn't think so!"

Once aloft we were doing some stalls, and I had failed to give sufficient rudder to compensate for the torque of the engine, when he suddenly stomped on the right rudder pedal and almost shouted, "Don't you ever use any rudder?" Needless to say, it wasn't much of a lesson, and I noticed he wasn't around the next time I came out.

The y-type instructor was encouraging. After explaining the situation before we got into the plane, he asked if there were any questions about the previous ground-school lesson. Then he affirmed whatever maneuvers he could, correcting what was necessary. He left me with a feeling that I wanted to be the best flyer I could. How I worked for that man! He created an attitude about flying that not only enabled me to manipulate an airplane but gave me a basis for determining when I should fly and when I shouldn't. There was a quiet authority in his teaching. He left no doubt about who was PIC (pilot in command), yet increasingly he encouraged me to make my own decisions and develop professional procedures. He was a servant to my emergence.

When Christ created each member of a family with creative potential, he didn't expect that potential to be buried under a blanket of restrictions or hidden in a closet of frustrations. No institution is better suited than the home to bring about human development, and that is the responsibility of the head of the house.

"Who's in charge here?" Jesus Christ. And in reverence to him, a husband—a servant-head to wife and children, sacrificing for their development—and a wife, exercising the authority that accompanies her gifts, ministering to her husband, her children, and her world, grow together with those in their household to be the exciting, liberated, and maturing persons the world is standing on tiptoe longing to see coming in their liberty!

3

Love Honors the Gift

THREE O'CLOCK in the afternoon is not my best time for
counseling. I suppose the problem is that my body considers it well past the time for a midday nap and refuses
to stand at the duty station. Sometimes it can be an
awful experience trying to keep my eyes open.

On one particular afternoon I looked with groggy
eyes at my date book to check on my next appointment.
I perked up immediately when I saw the names of a
young man and woman I had recently married. They
were a delightful couple who always left me with a
deposit of joy. Their premarital counseling had been a
happy experience for me. They were always full of
questions, and they explored new ideas and concepts
like a couple of avid mountain climbers attacking a new
peak. One of the agreements we made was that they
would come back from time to time to talk over their
growth, their ideas, and any problems they wanted to
share.

The next hour was no disappointment. Fred was
dressed casually in a nubby knit sweater, Marcia in her

granny-dress. Their eyes danced with joy; they were alive with a new idea! I wondered what it would be this time.

"Something you said in our premarital sessions meant a lot to us, and we have been trying to work it out. We think we have. Would you like to hear it?"

"Don't keep me in suspense," I said, as I motioned them toward a couch.

"You know how much Christ has meant to us and to the kids we work with in Young Life. Well, we have been discovering something about gifts of the Holy Spirit—in marriage, that is."

For the moment my mind turned to the charismatic emphasis that is alive in Washington: speaking in tongues, gifts of the Spirit such as prophecy and healing. But Fred and Marcia meant something else.

"We are discovering gifts in our marriage," Marcia explained. "Not roles determined strictly by sex, but by the abilities the Holy Spirit has given each of us."

"Oh, true enough," Fred chimed in, "I'm the head of the house. We believe the man should be the head of the house, just as Paul said. And yes, Marcia is going to have the babies. But in our counseling we liked the idea of my being a 'servant-head.' Like Christ, I want my authority to be used to help Marcia realize her gifts of the Spirit. And that goes for the little one, too," he said with a cat-ate-the-mouse look toward his wife.

"Is this some kind of announcement?" I queried.

"I guess so," she confirmed, "and we're thrilled about

it. What we are saying includes the baby, too. Can we
share this new insight with you?"

"Go ahead."

"Fred says he doesn't want me to give up my career
at the medical lab. We've decided on two children, and
of course I'm going to be a full-time mother while they
are young. But when they are in nursery school, I'll go
back to work part time. Fred and I agree that the children need both a mother and a father, so he is going to
take time to be with the kids each day. That will mean
some planning, such as where we are going to live. We
don't want Fred to live so far from work that commut-
ing eats up two hours a day. It will also mean limiting
our nighttime activities. We'll have to cut down on
some of our church work, so the kids won't be church
orphans."

"I feel the children need to experience tenderness
and care from a dad and not just from the mother,"
Fred said. "So it will be my job to bathe the tykes and
get them ready for bed, which will also give Marcia
relief at the end of the day. But on top of that, each of
these little ones will have some potential for development, and I want to share in the fun of finding out what
that is. Then I want to help them develop it. Maybe
that's selfish of me, but that's the way I feel."

"I think it's great!" I responded.

Perhaps Fred and Marcia are learning early in their
marriage what it had taken Colleen and me some years
to discover: when a person comes to Christ, one of the

most exciting things that happens is that he or she receives a gift, or gifts, of the Spirit. These gifts are meant
to be used for the common good in the body of Christ,
and the great joy of having them comes from knowing
that one has a place in the family of God. And who does
not need to be needed?

Gifts of the Spirit

A gift of the Spirit is an ability to fulfill a need in the
body of Christ. Whatever function is needed, the Spirit
designs a gift and gives it to a Christian. When we say
it is given for the common good, we mean it is to be
used for another's benefit.

God is a practical God who wants to see his children
provided for. He wants his body to function for the sake
of the lost world he still loves very much. When all the
parts are working properly, the body grows vigorously
and a deep interdependence emerges so that when one
member suffers, the whole body suffers together. If one
rejoices, all the parts rejoice together.

Obviously the gifts of the Spirit are given without
reference to sex. Just as there was no difference in the
dominion given to male and female in the Creation, so
there is no sex basis for receiving the gifts of the Spirit.
The Prophet Joel, foretelling the coming of the Holy
Spirit, predicted: "And it shall come to pass afterward,
that I will pour out my spirit on all flesh; your *sons* and
your *daughters* shall prophesy, your old men shall

dream dreams, and your young men shall see visions."
(Joel 2:28 RSV, italics mine).

Luke also speaks of the four daughters of Philip the
Evangelist exercising their gift of prophecy, which Paul
described as the highest of the gifts (*see* Acts 21:8).
Evidently the gifts of the Spirit were for both male and
female alike, with no distinction based on sex.

In the presently renewed interest in the gifts of the
Spirit, some have held rather strict interpretation as to
the number and identity of the gifts; some say there are
five gifts, some eight, and others claim twelve. Looking
at the varying lists Paul mentions, I do not believe he
was enumerating only so many gifts and no more. The
table below illustrates my point.

Lists of the Gifts of the Spirit

Romans 12:6–8	1 Corinthians 12:7–10	1 Corinthians 12:28	Ephesians
Prophecy	Wisdom	Apostles	Apostles
Service	Knowledge	Prophets	Prophets
Teaching	Faith	Teachers	Evangelists
Exhorting	Healing	Workers of	Pastors
Contributing	Miracles	Miracles	Teachers
Giving Aid	Prophecy	Healers	
	Discernment	Helpers	
	Tongues	Administrators	
	Interpretation of	Speakers in	
	Tongues	Tongues .	

I believe the apostle had in mind a broader meaning of the gifts based on the varying *needs* of the early church. God is wonderfully practical: if his church has a need, he gives some saint the ability to fill that need. If the needs change, so does his provision of the gifts. There must be a great deal of latitude in the broad categories designated "service," "helps," and "administration." The recipients of the latter must certainly have different roles today than in the early church. With our complex church structures, intricate budgets, tax complexities, personnel requirements, mechanical maintenance, and numerous details, I am sure the Lord has given some persons the ability to administer them in a complex age. I believe it because I have met such persons. If there is a need, God's Spirit creates a gift to meet that need. It is as broad and simple as that.

So it is with the home! God provides gifts of his Spirit within the home irrespective of sex—except, of course, for the obvious specialized ability of women to bear children, and of men to sire them, and perhaps a few others. Some women have the gift of financial management, and some husbands that of cooking; some women have the gift of spiritual teaching, and some husbands the gift of sensitive discernment. The thrill of a marriage is the continuous discovery of one another's gifts, and as the seasons of marriage change, so do some of the gifts.

Seasons may change the roles and gifts; circumstances may alter the gifts within a marriage.

We know a couple whose roles have been changed by a serious illness that left the husband semiparalyzed and unable to continue in his profession. His wife has gone to work and discovered gifts she never dreamed she had—resulting in a highly creative and successful career. The husband laughs about being a "house-husband," but seems to enjoy his new role. He has become a gourmet cook and runs their home like a pro. There is a sweetness in their relationship that comes, I believe, from their mutual submission to changing times and gifts.

Finance is an area many people think belongs in the husband's basket. But must it always be so? Suppose the husband doesn't have such a gift? In the home where I grew up, it was my mother who managed the finances. Even though Dad made the final decisions, it was Mother who supplied the data and the counsel by which those decisions were arrived at. I think God knew that he would use Dad in a way that would leave little time for anything other than his ministry, so he equipped Mother to manage the household finances.

Granted that God creates and provides the gifts, how, then, are we to discover them?

Gift Discovery

There probably will be little gift discovery unless the Christian is actively engaged in the body of Christ. We are not very good at discovering ourselves under isolated conditions. In our home, primarily, and then in the church and society, we discover who we are as we interrelate with others. Prayer may certainly be one of the methods, but seldom is prayer effective without some input from our brothers and sisters, the body of Christ.

For instance, one of the ways we discover who we are is through the *honesty* of others. The best illustration I have comes from my own life.

Administrative detail is *not* one of my gifts. Even on our wedding day I was working up to the last minute, barely getting ready in time for the ceremony. But Colleen had completed her work two days early and had rested and read! At times I let things go longer than I should. Oh, yes, I can plead the pressure of demands and all that sort of thing, but my wife gets things done quietly, quickly, and early.

At times Colleen will exercise her honesty and bring to my attention something that really needs to be done. I know I should be grateful, yet I'll have to admit that I resist her honesty, less now then previously, I must hurry to add. Her reminder touches my guilt buttons, and my lights of defensive reaction go on. But recently, as I have been submitting to her honesty, we have discovered one of her gifts in our marriage. It's what we might call "discerning administration," or an ability to sense what is important and then doing something about the matter without any last-minute hassles. This gift brings a sense of order to the body, whether in the church or in the home.

On the other side of the coin, Colleen takes no risks about physical safety, although she is very venturesome in life and philosophy. She wanted to keep that motherly protective ring around the children longer than I thought wise. One summer many years ago the children were striking out across a little lake near where our folks lived—a distance of about 400 yards—paddling plastic air mattresses like paddle boards. As Colleen stood on the dock, calling them back with desperate "mommy noises," the kids turned around and called back that they were okay. They were good swimmers and knew how to rest on their backs in the water. I was quite sure they would come to one another's aid should anything happen to one of the rafts. Besides, the motorboat was close at hand and ready to go. I had to pull rank on Coke and exercise my gift, which was turning the children loose to their adventuresome exploits. At times I had to encounter her about her overprotectiveness, and she is gracious enough to say that out of my honesty and her discovery of my gift, she has been able to let go.

Sensitive communication is a second way in which we discover our gifts. It happened to a pastor and his wife whose three active children had kept them busy and on their toes for years. Then the time came when the children left home, and the pastor's life settled down to the dull roar of administering one of the country's most creative churches. But something crucial had gone out of the home for the wife. Restlessness began to stalk her peace; an edge of sharpness replaced her patient, reserved behavior. Because her husband was a sensitive and caring person, these changes did not escape his notice, and soon he was drawing his wife out in conversation. At first she felt pangs of guilt because she was dissatisfied with the usual role of a minister's wife. But her husband kept drawing out her feelings, saying they were more important than prescribed roles. "I'm married to you, not to the church," he said. As the wife allowed her feelings to flow, she and her husband began to realize that she was interested in counseling. Her desire to be involved in therapy was so strong that she felt she wanted to work at a professional level. That meant a great deal of training, but with her husband's encouragement, she became a schoolgirl again—in her mid-forties. She sailed through her B.A. degree, lighthearted as a lark. Her M.A. was captured with honors, and she trudged on toward her doctorate. It took years, but she did it. At times the stress took its toll upon their relationship, but they always talked things out, made the adjustments, and forged ahead. Now the wife has opened an office and has a very effective ministry of her own as she conducts her own therapeutic practice. And it all began with her husband's encouraging her to talk out what she felt—exercising the gift of sensitive communication.

Helping another person to get out what he or she is feeling *is* a gift. It's like "pulling the web out of the spider," which is a phrase I have to explain with a story.

As a boy I loved football; it was in my genes—the ones I got from Dad. Whenever we could, he and I went down to the Pitt Stadium to watch Pitt or Carnegie Tech play. One morning I had walked the two miles from our house to the church to meet my father, who had been counseling. A young man was just leaving as I knocked on the study door. For a moment we three stood on the steps leading out of my father's study, its gothic vault rising high overhead in light oak and its leaded windows letting in the soft light of a cool November day. A spider decided to make his appearance in our midst, hanging from his web right before our faces. The young man reached up, took the web and said, "Watch." Down, down, down went the spider until he had almost reached the floor, vainly struggling to gather in his web faster than it was being extricated from him. The young man took my hand and said, "Here, you try it." I shook the web, but too gently. The spider was gaining on me! Almost frantically I increased the sharpness of my shaking. Suddenly the web broke. Without a moment's delay, my friend picked up the web and got things going again. Then he took my hand and gave me the right rhythm and intensity. Out came the web, longer and longer.

Getting a person to talk about his feelings is like shaking the web out of a spider. Too gently and he gets it all back inside. Too brusquely and the web of communication breaks. There is that gentle but persistent touch that helps one to get out what the other person is feeling. And as the other talks, an interest may begin to emerge. Like the web of a spider, a latent desire may be extracted.

Love honors the gift potential and listens.

A third way of discovering others' gifts is to "mirror" another person's strengths, to reflect back to the other affirmatively what we feel his or her gift to be.

A couple Colleen and I came to know very well in seminary was a good example of the "mirroring of affirmation." The husband had been very successful in his business for over eleven years, but a kind of restlessness pervaded all he did. His work didn't have the zing he needed.

The wife began to watch for her husband's high points, those moments of joy that gave him the greatest fulfillment. They turned out to be people-moments—occasions when, through his sensitivity, he was able to give insight to one of his colleagues. With a deft and smooth firmness he would bring warring parties together and inspire them to settle disputes. When it came to sharing his faith, he had a modern, down-to-earth reasonableness about him that was regularly bringing people to Christ. As his wife began to mirror back his high points, helping him to compare them with the low points of his business life, a mound of data began to grow. One day he said, "You know what, honey?—I just might go into the ministry. What would you think of that? Scare ya?"

His wife had been raised in a Swedish pastor's family. She knew the pressures and struggles, the leannesses and the tough times; but she knew there would be a deep satisfaction for her man. "No," she said, "it doesn't scare me a bit! You'd make a great minister. Darling, I'm with you a hundred percent, and I'm ready to start tomorrow!"

He decided to take a couple of days off to pray about it. He drove to his favorite retreat, a place where the fish played exciting games with lures before they struck. The second afternoon, after a good catch, a time of prayer, and a leisurely nap in the woods, he "woke up in the ministry." He was one of the most relaxed, effective pastors I have known.

In our own family I can see the children going to Colleen for their heart-sharing; but they come to me for counsel on their religion or history papers. They are helping us to identify our gifts by "mirroring re- sponses" to our strengths.

One more factor in the discovery of gifts is the will- ingness to *allow another to risk*. Discovery cannot take place unless there is an "atmosphere of permission"— a language that says, "Try it, see if it is for real."

A couple we knew many years ago did this, and it worked well for them. Betsey had been a nesting bird all through her marriage. Nothing gave her greater joy than providing for her husband and their children. But now that the two children were ready to "fly the nest," she was becoming progressively depressed. Finally she descended into a state that required hospitalization for a few days.

Betsey's husband was warmly sensitive and supportive during the recovery period as her anxiety rose and fell like waves. He helped her disengage from a number of her civic activities and affirmed her desire to work with her hands. Her sewing was full of creative and innovative ideas; cleverness of design marked everything she did. A mixture of practicality and striking art made her products go like hot cakes at bazaars. She thought of starting a gift shop, but her low self-image took care of that! She had almost no sense of self-worth. "Try it," her husband would say. "Don't bite the whole thing off at once, but work in someone else's shop for a while to see if you like it." So she got a part-time job, and he drove her to the shop three times a week. Bit by bit her assurance began to grow; she tried it and she liked it! Without her husband's encouragement, she probably would have stayed in her cave, peering fearfully out at a world where she saw others playing joyfully at the things they liked. But with one who loved her saying, "Try it," she found the strength and "took a cut at it." She discovered a gift—and a new business to boot . . . one that through the years has blessed her —and others.

Gift Development

Once love aids in the process of discovery, the next phase of *gift development* gets underway. Love provides resources for the development of another's gift.

In a previous chapter we spoke of the type of leadership that is essential for gift development. In the home the husband is the head, and if he is exercising the y (or servant)-style of leadership, he will not only permit but will stimulate the growth of others in his home. Because gifts have their own authority, he will allow other members of the family to *exercise the authority* that accompanies their gift.

Colleen has the gift of "pacing," and when she uses it she does so with an authority I must take seriously. My natural tendency is to run the "ship" at full speed all of the time. Needless to say, the whole crew gets worn out, and so does the skipper. And when the skipper gets worn out, he reacts in ways that can make shipboard life a hassle. It's about that time that the senior medical officer comes charging out of her stateroom, resolutely mounts the ladder to the bridge and says, "Captain, slow this vessel down! In fact, put into port for a few days! We all need some R and R." And believe me, I have learned to follow the advice of the "medical officer." She knows whereof she speaks!

Another way in which love resources development is by *providing time* for the other person to exercise his or her gift. A husband, or wife for that matter, can be so demanding of the other's time that any possibility of gift development is buried under a mountain of things to do. And buried deeply! In fact, this can become a means of keeping a mate from the development of a potential.

To give Colleen an opportunity to cultivate her writing ability, the children and I had to decrease our demands on her time. She felt she needed quiet times in which to create—not little crumbs of minutes here and there but solid blocks of hours when an idea could grow without being scorched by the searing winds of constant demands. She thought Tuesdays and Thursdays were the best times. On Mondays she would get a good start on the week and clear up a lot of home and administrative details. Wednesdays she saved for church interests. On Thursdays I was at the church with the staff all day, which cut off any chance of our getting together. But her new routine meant no guests for dinner on Tuesday or Thursday nights, otherwise another gift of hers, that of hospitality, would demand spending half the day preparing for the guests. So, no surprises on Tuesdays or Thursdays! No phone calls at the last minute to ask, "How about a few extras for dinner tonight?" Okay on other days, but Tuesdays and Thursdays were "no-nos."

Financial resources are often necessary for the development of another's gifts, and love makes the sacrifice to free them. Fen was a notably successful doctor. He and Joyce had four college-age children. Gradually Joyce felt a lifelong ambition catching fire again—she wanted to become a high-level administrative assistant. She knew she had the problem-solving abilities and the public relations "savvy" to do the job. But training would be needed. That meant money, and a fair amount at that, for tuition at a top-flight executive training institute!

"Any chance, Fen?" she asked timidly.

"Honey, no way," he retorted without hesitation. "We couldn't afford it. You know that!"

That was just the point: Joyce knew differently. She kept Fen's books. She saw as much as $17,000 go down the drain one month for repairs to his yacht, and there was the light, twin-engine aircraft he maintained for his own pleasure. Month after month Joyce made out checks totaling several thousand dollars to pay for Fen's "playing." He had plenty of chances to put the boat and the plane on lease-back arrangements, but he insisted that he "might want them at a moment's notice" and so held on to them like a little boy selfishly guarding his toys. Out of a $150,000-a-year practice, he could not break loose $5,000 to a wife who was doing at least a $15,000-a-year job of business and financial management for him, to say nothing of writing some of his medical speeches and papers.

On top of that, Fen dallied and reneged on so many promises to support the children in their advanced education that they failed to get into school and had to work to save enough money to go to school. Now, I'm for children working to help with their educational expenses, but the communication that came through loud and clear from Fen was "After me, you come *third!*"

Today Fen has left his family and is still running around like a teenager trying to find himself. His wife has accomplished her goal and is carrying out a great ministry for God, but not without the pain of rejection still throbbing in her life. Fen was not about to provide resources for her as a person—much less work toward the development of her gift.

One of the greatest stimuli to development is good old *encouragement* or *affirmation*. In the marriage ceremony there is a question asked of the couple: "[so and so], will you have this [woman/man] to be your [wife/husband] and will you pledge your troth to [her/him] in all love and honor, in all duty and service, in all *faith* and tenderness?" The assenting parties are then to say, "I will."

In using the word *faith*, I mean not only fidelity in the sexual relationship but faith *in the person.* "I know you can make it" are the magic words that give many of us the courage to try and keep trying. And they may have to be said many times. For someone to throw up his hands and say, "Oh, there's no use! You'll never make it!" is one of the most rejecting, demotivating things that can happen to a person. True, some of us take that as an extra stimulus and try all the harder to prove ourselves. The only trouble is, we seldom quit trying to prove, and our whole life becomes a game of "I told you I could!" When I see someone putting others down in ruthless competition, I can't help but feel that there has been precious little faith-input logged into the computer of that person's disposition.

The term *faith-input* reminds me of a pastor's family in Pittsburgh, Pennsylvania. They lived in the simplest circumstances, close by the car line where the pastor

could take the streetcar to the church most days. The
parents saw their two hard-working children through
medical school and music conservatory by living fru-
gally, borrowing whenever necessary sums that took
them years to repay. Only in their later years were they
able to buy a humble house in the older section of Los
Angeles where the pastor's ministry ended. But my,
they were proud of that house! And the children are
two people who know very well the joy and solid foundation of a love that sacrificed for their emergence.
Love had honored the gifts and resourced them.

Gifts and talents, in the broad sense, are meant to be
used, not only in the body of the church but also within
marriage. Strict rules determined by sex or tradition
can stifle. But the Spirit—and the gifts that equip us for
life and ministry—can bring creative fulfillment, har-
mony, and joy.

4

This Is Where I Am— Where Are You?

IT WAS SUNDAY . . . a beautiful spring evening in the hills of Bel Air, California. The scent of night-blooming jasmine came through the open windows on the wings of a gentle breeze, and it seemed that all was well in the world.

I was getting ready for the evening service of the new church Louie had been sent to Bel Air to start. I was standing in front of the big mirror in our bathroom, brushing my hair. I remember hearing the front door open and close as people began to congregate in our living room as they did each Sunday night. Louie had been out making calls on new members, and now I heard him open the sliding glass door into our bedroom —no doubt slipping in the back way so he could catch his breath and wash up before facing the nearly one hundred people sitting in our front room.

Our life since arriving in Bel Air had been a fast track —I mean, *really!* . . . A constant round of calls, meet-

ings, and people. It wasn't that we were never together
—just so rarely *alone.* It had been weeks since we had
had an evening for ourselves. I was tired. We had four
babies under five years of age, and a home that doubled
as a church office, sanctuary, and fellowship hall. But
more than being tired, I was in some strange way
lonely. Not that I didn't love our work. I was as excited
about it as Louie was . . . and our people were marvelous. But something was wrong, and I was just beginning
to wrestle with whatever it was.

At that point, enter Louie. There he was, standing
beside me, washing his hands. He was excited about the
call he had just made, thrilled with what God was doing
in the lives of people in our fellowship, and eagerly
planning the next project to move on to in the church
—and the next, and the next.

Now, at that point, as the good wife, I of course
shared his enthusiasm—right? Wrong! The more he
talked and the more excited he became, the more I
grappled with my churning insides. My feelings rose
higher and higher, that lump in my throat got bigger,
and finally the tears spilled over the top, and I let him
have it. Poor Louie! All those people in the living room
waiting to be inspired, and his wife dissolves in tears in
the bathroom. But he listened, and I'll always be grateful to him for that.

I'm not sure exactly what I said, but between sniffs
and sobs I was somehow able to tell Louie about the
need I was just beginning to sense within myself. I told

him how hungry I was to be with him, to have time to talk and dream, alone. I shared my strong feeling that there had to be a change in our relentless schedule, a change that would give us time to communicate and build our relationship.

Well, there obviously wasn't time for Louie to hear me out completely just then, but later—after the meeting was over and the door had closed for the last time —he did. We sat and talked for a very long time, saying things we both wanted and needed to hear—things we had been almost too busy to think, much less say to one another. I remember Louie thanked me for being honest about my feelings—and that meant something special to me. He also agreed that indeed we did need to slow down in order to have time to nurture our own relationship.

And then he did a simple, practical—and, to me, very beautiful—thing. He took his little date book from his pocket, and looked until he found a free night. It happened to be Thursday of the following week, and he said, "That's our night." And so it was the next week that we had an evening all to ourselves. Out of that night came a decision to put aside time every week for the same purpose . . . and so it has been in all the years since . . . Thursday night.

Now I'm sure many couples are able to *find* time for each other in an easy, unscheduled way, and that's wonderful. But that didn't work for us. With our kind of life we found we had to *make* time—not that we would always be able to adhere to it rigidly—literally grabbing hold of our schedules and writing it into our date books. And that was one of the most important decisions we ever made . . . the decision to *make* time to say, "This is where I am, where are you?" For any marriage, or any relationship of depth, will only be as good as its communication. And communication takes time!

It also takes being *aware* of where you are, for communication is not just talking *to,* or *at* someone. It is a sharing of real feelings. . . . what we think, feel, value —what we fear, hate—what we dream about and believe in.

Communication is part of being an authentic person . . . we say what we feel and feel what we say. Of course, we do not communicate only through our words. We communicate in many different ways at the same time, so that even the sharing of a few words can send a very complicated message. In fact, whether we speak or not, in an intimate relationship we are constantly sending and receiving messages. We can speak volumes with a look, a tone of voice, a touch on the shoulder as we pass our partner's chair at the family table. A person who truly communicates will "match" inside and out. As we grow in our ability to communicate in marriage we can help each other to become authentic people—we can know ourselves better and match inside and out. For in a way I must be able to share who I am transparently with my husband in order to *know* who I am.

The cry for communication is loud and persistent!

Among the women I know, I hear this hunger expressed more than any other: "If only my husband would talk to me!" "We just *don't* communicate." Or, "He's so busy making money! I don't want his money, I want *him!*"

Women are hungry for their men . . . hungry to know and be known. But it doesn't go only one way. Men, too, have this basic desire, and how healthy it is that our society is finally granting its permission for men to express their needs openly. The drive we feel to know and be known is not linked to our sex but to our basic humanity. We want it so much because God created us to have it.

So many couples begin marriage convinced that nothing will take away the closeness they feel, and somehow they miss the truth that love and communication go hand in hand and must be worked at—or else, like unused muscles, they will atrophy from disuse. I'm thinking of a couple we know. They were ecstatic when they first got married . . . and they were happy for a few years. He enjoyed his work, she enjoyed being at home with the children. They looked forward to seeing each other at the end of each day. On weekends they had fun together. Then very gradually it all began to change. At night when he came home they found themselves saying the same things to each other. He was preoccupied, and she felt she was intruding when she asked him questions about his job. Yet she wanted so much to talk to him! All day, every single day, she was with the

children. They lived in a very small town where nothing exciting seemed to happen, and she longed for him
to tell her what went on in the city where people were
busy doing interesting things. She tried to make conversations of her own, but what could she talk about
except the people she saw at the supermarket or how
her dime got stuck in the dry cleaning machine. Finally
one evening he snapped, "I don't want to hear about
that stuff! It's boring!" He might just as well have said
she was boring—and maybe she was. His work and the
people he met were so fascinating—how could she
keep up with them?

That happens to a lot of marriages. According to
some psychiatrists, the average man and wife communicate with each other for twenty-eight minutes a
week. They may talk a lot more than that, and they may
transmit messages in ways other than verbal, but obviously they aren't getting through to each other. And if
they aren't getting through, they aren't communicating!

That reminds me of something Paul Tournier wrote:
"Listen to all the conversations of our world, between
nations as well as those between couples. They are for
the most part dialogues of the deaf."

So that we do not join forces with the "dialoguing
deaf," we need to work on our communication in marriage, and as we do, the life and teachings of Jesus will
be a real help. He was so direct, so transparent, yet
always so full of care for the other person. When he

said, "Let your yes be yes, and your no be no," he was guiding us toward simplicity, clarity, and frankness. Some people call it *truthing it*—that is, *speaking the truth in love*. This is a term used in David Augsburger's *The Love Fight.*

Lately, in my own life, as I've been working on *truthing,* I have been trying to learn to speak more accurately. It's too easy for me to say "others feel," when what I really mean is "I feel." I also have noticed that when Louie and I are talking, I am inclined to want to speak for him—"I feel you feel that I feel." In my journey toward transparency, I would like to let others speak for themselves, and I accept the responsibility I have to speak for myself. This is part of *truthing it*— and *truthing it* is good for communication.

But *truthing it* is not just speaking the truth . . . it is also *hearing* the truth, in love . . . being open to the truth about ourselves. And this is another area on which I need to work. When I listen, I want to hear *truly.* I don't want to block out what my husband—or others— might be trying to say to me simply because they are saying things I might not like to hear.

When I listen to my husband, I want to hear what *he* feels—not what I feel about him. Not hearing feelings can be a stumbling block in the way of being a true listener. I remember a time in our marriage when Louie was feeling particularly inadequate about his work. He really doubted his teaching and preaching ability, and it was a painful period for him. He tried to tell me what he was feeling, but I thought he was so gifted, so strong in these areas, that I couldn't hear him when he said he was hurting. My repeated affirmations —"I'd rather listen to you preach than anyone" . . . "I learn so much when you teach"—fell on deaf ears. What I felt *about* him was getting in the way of my hearing *him*. Finally he convinced me. To my amazement I saw that at that time and place he really *did* feel inadequate. It was only then I was able to hear him, to feel *with* him, and to walk with him during a dark time.

Another very real part of communication is conflict —and learning how to talk and work through difficult problems. In a wonderful little book called *Why Am I Afraid to Tell You Who I Am?* by John Powell, I came across this statement:

> All deep and authentic friendships, and especially the union of those who are married, must be based on absolute openness and honesty. At times, gut-level communication will be most difficult, but it is at these precise times that it is necessary. Among close friends or between partners in marriage there will come from time to time a complete emotional and personal union.

I agree. Gut-level communication *is* risky, but if a couple have enough faith in the strength of their relationship, they can take the risk. The greater risk is to avoid it out of fear of conflict.

If we are still battling the fear of being rejected, we

will see conflict as a crushing threat—"If we clash, you may reject me." Most marriages have to grow in their ability to handle conflicts in a natural way . . . as partners grow in the security of their love and commitment, they are able to venture and risk without fear. Some partners begin marriage with the understanding that honesty and criticism will not only be allowed but will be encouraged in their relationship.

In his sensitive book *I Loved a Girl* Walter Trobisch writes:

> Before he was married, one of my friends wrote to his fiancée about what he expected from his future wife: . . . "She must challenge me to the highest degree by completely honest criticism of me. . . . When she is disappointed in me, she must not withdraw her confidence. . . . She must never pretend, but must tell me honestly when I have hurt her."
>
> Do you understand? What he wanted was not a servant girl, but an equal partner who stands beside him before God. Only with such a partner can you become "one flesh" in the real depths of its meaning—a new, living being. Partnership includes the right to criticize.

Of course, there are different ways to confront and criticize . . . and different times! For instance, I know better than to mention something like that on the night before Louie has to preach a sermon.

The point is, conflict doesn't need to be bad—it is natural. It is precisely because marriage is such a close intimate relationship that it also has such a high susceptibility for conflict. But it can even be fun when it's dealt with as quickly as possible, openly and with love and respect. Of course, conflict can be painful, too, but even when it is, we should not fear it or run from it. How we handle our hassles, how we work through our differences and conflicts, tells much about the kind of people we are and the way we live. It also tells us something about our philosophy and the goals for our marriage. If peace is our objective, we may not risk conflict. If a creative relationship is our desire, we must.

In working through problems and conflicts there are some steps, or dynamics, of communication that can be helpful. Because they have worked for people we know —and for us—I would like to share them in the hope that they will be useful to someone else in a time of need. I like them, not because they are foolproof (they're not), but because they offer partners the opportunity to minister to one another in the process.

First, if one partner is really troubled by a problem or situation, the other partner has to resist counterattacking and just hold his tongue for a while. That does not mean he becomes a doormat or a target for abuse. Perhaps for a short time he has to be dumped on, but the important thing is that he gives the other person a chance to unburden himself.

The listener in this case is the minister to the other.

Sometimes he may have to try to extract whatever it is that has built up inside the other. Perhaps a husband needs to communicate that he's having a painfully hard time with his boss. Perhaps a wife is troubled by an interfering mother, or she may be having problems with *her* boss. Maybe something in their relationship is painful. Whatever it is, it has to come out, and it never will if both partners are wounding each other with their angry barbs.

When the listening partner feels that the other has finally gotten it all out, that's the time for him to go back over the same ground, asking, "Is this how you feel? Am I getting it right?" He is not agreeing with the other person, he is trying to determine where the other person is. Perhaps the other partner will have to correct him a few times, but finally the listener should be able to say, "Yes, I understand."

Second, now that the dark river has begun to dissipate, the clear stream of insight can begin to flow. The listener continues to listen, giving the other partner the freedom to explore the causes and sources of his anger. It's important for the listener to refrain from making any suggestions of his own. Let the other person identify his own problems, difficult and halting as that may be.

Third, once a partner knows what is bothering him he can begin to consider alternative solutions. Again, the listening partner shouldn't try to impose answers on him, although he can help to explore the solutions open to the other person. If a boss is domineering, or if a mother is the kind who tries to tell a wife how to bring up her children, what can the other person do about it? And what might the outcome be? Perhaps these same alternatives occurred to the troubled person earlier, but because he couldn't articulate them they seemed too risky. Now that he is able to talk about them with an understanding listener, they may seem totally different to him. Perhaps a husband will decide that he wants to change his job. Or he may decide that he can handle his anger without taking it out on his wife. Perhaps a wife may decide that there is a way she can encounter her mother without destroying the relationship. And at this point perhaps one partner may be able to say to the other, "Honey, just the fact that I'm talking this out with you makes me feel better."

Fourth, any decision made immediately after an outburst of anger should be reconsidered later. Sometimes, in the wake of an emotional explosion, a person is so eager to compromise that he may regret his decision later. So, after a day or two, the listening partner should talk over the decision with him, asking, "Is this what you meant? Is this what we agreed to do?" If the other person has second thoughts, the decision should be altered to include them.

Fifth, okay—each partner knows how the troubled one is going to deal with the source of his anger. What then? Is the problem solved? Will there never be another outburst over this same issue? Not on your life!

Here is where the ministering partner must be *patient* and *prayerful* . . . two of the best ways to support the one he loves.

Usually problems are caused by deep habit patterns. If we human beings were able to change direction on a dime, our lives would be so different. But because many of our responses are conditioned over long periods of time, our old habits usually linger for a while after we begin asking God to break us free of them. As Corrie ten Boom says, "After you stop ringing a bell, there may be a few *dings* left." No matter how vehemently one partner proclaims that he is going to change his behavior, there's the chance he'll get into the same rut again—possibly again and again.

What does the ministering partner do when that happens? Does he say, "You dope! You blew it!"? Not if he has faith in the other person's potential. Instead of making the other partner feel like a failure because he goofed, the ministering partner says, "Hey, I'm hanging in there with you. I know it's tough, but I'm praying with you, and with God's help, I know you can do it." And when the day comes that the old response gives way to a new one, no one is more grateful than the ministering partner.

This process of communication is one more way of submitting to one another out of reverence for Christ . . . submitting to the need of one partner to be heard and understood. In the last twenty-five years Louie has submitted to me many times—and I to him—in this

way. We don't take turns or keep score. It happens
when it needs to happen. It takes time, emotional energy, and patience on the part of the listener, but the
reward of SHALOM (the real peace that comes after
struggle) is worth it all. As one couple who have grown
in their ability to share deeply put it: "Now we can talk
as two human beings instead of paper dolls labeled
'wife' and 'husband.' "

Communication is work; it is costly; but it is one of the
best investments any of us who are married can make.

> I love you
>
> If I love you
> I must tell you the truth
>
> I want your love
> I want your truth
>
> Love me enough to
> Tell me the truth.

> DAVID W. AUGSBURGER

5

Seven Basics
of a Happy Marriage

IT HAPPENED AGAIN, just the other day. A couple married for several years came in for counseling. They wanted to save their marriage, yet they were beginning to think they never should have married in the first place. Neither was living up to the other's expectations. Each one had become someone "different from what I had imagined." In a sense, the more they knew of one another, the more they became strangers.

I'm not sure that love is blind, but infatuation certainly is. In the early stages of a relationship a man and a woman are so caught up in the excitement of a new personality and in the sexual attractions they feel for each other that they don't see each other clearly. Sometimes they create images of the other person, and then marry the image rather than the real person. Illusion pushes honesty out of the picture.

The romantic attraction of one person for another can be deceptive; it can keep you from knowing the

"real" person. That is why there is such a thing as courtship. It is not a useless ritual, nor is it a period of en-
forced frustration conceived by puritanical parents. At
least it should not be.

Ideally, courtship should allow a couple to work their
way through the blur of infatuation toward the sharper
focus of reality. This is their opportunity to get to know
one another as the man or woman each truly is. And,
more important, this is that critical time when they can
discover whether or not they can achieve a life together. Courtship must be an honest appraisal by two
people trying to discover their basis for a realistic marriage.

My counseling experience has taught me that there
are several basic areas in which a man and woman must
agree if they are to have the highest quality marriage.
I have chosen seven basics to discuss here: religion, sex,
finance, children, friends, home, and goals. It is not
absolutely essential for a couple to agree completely on
all of them—the engine runs with missing cylinders but
not so smoothly or powerfully. However, because these
areas arouse such strong feelings in all of us, I feel a
couple will be in for trouble if they basically disagree in
one or more of them.

When infatuation ends—and it always does—a couple must live in these areas of reality. How sad it is if
their discovery of one another becomes a disappointment, a sudden shattering of the fantasy each had built
around the other. And how much better if a couple can

reveal themselves honestly and courageously before making a lifelong commitment. Such courage and honesty may be difficult, but it is also part of becoming mature. The pain of realizing that they have basic differences is better borne before a man and a woman marry. Otherwise, not knowing who they are, they may be crushed by the way they seem to change later on.

We human beings are always in process of change—and that can work in our favor. If a man and a woman are not completely in agreement about the bases of their relationship as they begin their marriage, they can grow closer together. If they can communicate their ideas and feelings honestly and maturely, the process of change can bring them to new agreements.

This chapter is designed to aid couples to take a look at these seven areas where it is important to have agreement. I hope that it will stimulate couples to attempt to become more deeply and realistically acquainted with each other. As agreements and discrepancies are identified, they should be faced with a mixture of love and honesty.

The following steps will help you to explore these areas:

1. Set aside a definite period of time to be alone and undisturbed together.

2. Read aloud the section on one area of the seven basics.

3. Each should write a "profile of feelings" on that area and compare it with his partner's "profile."

4. After this exchange of feelings, each person should try to the best of his or her ability to understand the feelings of the other.

5. You are now face-to-face with your agreements and/or differences. How you cope with the differences is going to be a highly individual matter, and you will be influenced by your openness to one another, the depth of your differences, the intensity of your feelings, and the time necessary to make adjustments. If nothing else comes of this time together, you are certainly going to know each other a lot better.

Religion

Religion arouses the deepest emotions of the human personality. Even those who look down their noses at religion usually are the first to say that it has been the cause of some of man's bitterest wars. And that is the point!

Bring a strong difference of religion into a marriage, where both husband and wife have had significant religious conditioning, and there is indeed the makings for "war." If, on the other hand, one or both of the couple have had no particular depth of feeling about religion, any differences will probably be mild and cause little irritation.

Why all the emotion about religion?

The answer lies in the meaning of religion. The word *religion* means "that to which one is bound." Religion, therefore, is that to which we are tied or bound, determining what we live for; religion indicates our direction and determines our priorities. In the long run, our deepest motivations are determined by religion. True, sexual desire may determine short-term action, but over the long haul, it is religion that shapes our lives.

What do I mean by *religion?*

Try visualizing yourself on a sinking ship. You can take only one thing with you! What will it be? Your choice indicates your religion. That is what you are tied to. Religion is that for which you will give up all other things in life.

What will *you* give up other things for? What is the one thing you will *not* give up for anything else? That is your religion.

I usually ask a couple to try this exercise: Elbow out some time, curl up with each other, and share whatever it is that is most important to you. That will be your religion.

Now, what was it?—security, love of your spouse, money, the children (present or future), your home, position, success, influence, community status, God, Jesus Christ and his Kingdom?

Did you religions agree?

If not, hang on to your hat, because unless some sort of agreement can be reached, each of you will be tugging madly in different directions for the control of the limited resources of your lives: time, money, energy, and affection. And because the motivations are so primal, these tugs-of-war could create tensions that will be more than the marriage can handle.

Suppose one of you wishes to give large amounts of time, energy, or money to Christ's work and the church —but the other wishes those same resources spent on the social scene, the country club, and the business ladder. In spite of your compromises, you will miss the thrill of unity, and very likely you will experience a rift of emotions.

Religion is a growing experience, and the growth demands a means of expression. Now it's true that we know some couples where both partners have a deep personal faith in Christ—yet they worship and express their faith in different traditions and still have a real sense of spiritual oneness and growth in their home and marriage. However, couples such as this—in my experience—are the exceptions. Generally, if a couple cannot *go* together to church, they most likely will not *grow* together spiritually. And that will be a serious loss!

The other night Colleen and I attended a party where we met the charming wife of a young professional man. She had just had a religious experience that had made considerable changes in her life and feelings. Her husband did not attend church with her. He left her and their children to "do their religious thing" which, I felt, he thought was for "little old ladies and children and not red-blooded American men." The wife's pain and sense of loneliness were marked and rather tragic. Something which for many couples had been a bonding, deepening influence had become a point of raised eyebrows and ridicule in their marriage. That is one of the most painful and damaging interactions that can strike a couple's relationship.

Some couples, sensing their deep differences in religion, try to make deals or strike compromises—"Dr. Evans, we have it all worked out. On one Sunday we'll go to his church, on the other Sunday we'll go to my church. We'll let the children make up their own minds when they come of age."

Some deal! First of all, neither one can really put his or her heart into the religion of his choice, because that would put too much strain on the other. The agreement has hobbled both in their religious growth, and when something does not grow it becomes stagnant. The couple also have put their children in a very awkward position. First, they will ask their children to choose one religion over another without having much orientation in either. Another burden is that when they ask the children to choose one of their religions, it is very much like asking them to choose between Mom or Dad. And what child wants to do that? Usually the children do nothing, walk off into a religious wasteland, and raise their children as little pagans. By this time the religion that once was somebody's experience has become a convention, then an inconvenience, and finally totally irrelevant—all because of a "deal." Thank God, many young people sense the bankruptcy of such agreements and take seriously their religious commitments, being mature enough to grapple with the meaning of difference early in the game.

In some marriages where there is strong disagreement about religion one of the couple converts. Usually this happens when one partner feels very strongly about his or her religion and the other, sensing this and not having strong feelings of his or her own, says, "Okay, I'll convert." Sometimes it is an honest conversion, and the couple know the joy of religious unity in the marriage. Great! But in too many instances the scene goes something like this: Party A converts to Party B's religion—and unconsciously slips a card up his or her sleeve. Years go by. Then comes a struggle over a decision where apparently someone is going to have to give in. Slowly Party A's hand goes up the sleeve and pulls out the trump card. "Remember when I converted to your religion? Now it is your turn to convert to my opinion!" Usually this is not agreeable to Party B, who considers it both unfair and irrelevant. It is!

Sometimes one of the partners agrees to raise the children in the other's faith. Once I was called into a gorgeous home overlooking the Pacific Ocean from the high ridges of Bel Air, California. The wife had been a Roman Catholic, although not a very active one since their marriage. The husband had been an Episcopalian. They decided to compromise and come to a Presbyterian church. (I still can't see how the Presbyterians stand halfway between the Episcopalians and the Roman Catholics!) When their first child was of educable age, the wife suddenly felt deep pangs of guilt for not raising her child in the Roman Catholic faith. Her husband reminded her of her agreement, and I shall never forget the tragic truth of her response: "Yes, but I didn't realize what I was doing."

Of course, she didn't! Intellectually, she had made an agreement, an honest one, but without realizing that the conditioning and training we receive as children find deep roots in the religious furrows of our hearts. Just because we chop off the top portion of the plant and clear the field by some rational decision, that does not mean that the rootstock is dead. It may still be very active and able to come strongly to life under the right conditions. The religious training of the children was all the stimulation this woman's roots needed.

When religion is a matter of agreement, it can be a unifying and healing power in a marriage. A husband and wife who know Christ sense their acceptance by God as the Holy Spirit pours into their lives. It undergirds them with a deep sense of security, and several things happen. First, they both receive a basic affirmation from God's own Spirit, which gives them an assurance of acceptance by Someone very important to them. Then, the couple have a powerful Other to whom they can relate when they have differences. Neither must come to the place of the other; each can walk to a higher third position. As they come closer to Christ, they come closer to each other.

Years ago, when Colleen and I lived in Los Angeles,

we occasionally got tickets to the Rose Bowl game. We loved to park our car on the golf course, eat a picnic lunch with friends, and then walk over to the stadium. I would always give Colleen her ticket so that if we got separated in the jostling crowd, we could end up at the same place. I would always say, "Honey, in case we get separated, I'll meet you at tunnel so and so."

Once we *did* get separated! For a moment I felt waves of anxiety come over me as I found myself muttering, "What am I going to do now?" Then my last words to Colleen rang in my ears: "I'll meet you at tunnel so and so." When I got to the tunnel I stood on tiptoe, craning my neck to look over the crowd in hopes of finding Coke. There she came, pushed and shoved by the fast-moving crowd, smiling at those who apologized for bumping into her, her hand raised to hold her little knitted cap on her head. We had ended up at the same place.

When a Christian couple get separated by differences of opinion, each can always say, "Honey, I'll meet you at the feet of Christ." Neither has to come to the place of the other; nobody has to "win." Instead, each makes whatever corrections are necessary to bring him or her to the feet of Christ, and the closer they come to him, the closer they come to one another.

Sex

A couple I know always tell sex-oriented jokes. However, in private counseling sessions, the wife told me she thought intercourse was the "goring of an innocent victim." Unable to find satisfaction in her relationship with her husband, she constantly tries to bring other men and women together, often without regard for their marital status. Disruption follows in her wake all too many times. If this woman and her husband could have talked out their feelings about sex prior to their marriage, perhaps they could have done something about her unfortunate attitude. But to have talked about such things would have been "improper" in the sexual atmosphere in which this couple was raised.

I do not feel it is at all improper for a couple in their maturing relationship to talk about sex and its meaning to each of them. I would hope they would ask each other such questions as "What was the sexual atmosphere of your home? How do you think your mother and father felt about sex? In what ways did they indicate their joy or embarrassment about it? How did you come to know 'the facts of life'?" (The answer to that last question might be good for some real laughs if the parents were like many people in explaining about the "birds and the bees.")

My first awareness of sex with Colleen was characterized by a deep sense of communication. Having both experienced a new relationship with Christ, we gave our new relationship with each other to him. He would have us "save ourselves" for marriage, and we felt and knew that would take all the strength we had—and more—so we determined to lean heavily on God and accept from him the "strength for all things" he has promised. We wanted our physical expression to be an honest manifestation of our total relationship. We did not want to allow the sexual expressions to get out in front of the remainder of our relationship, nor did we want them to lag behind. (I must say, the latter was far easier than the former!) We felt that when we were ready "to go all the way" we would "go all the way in *every* way," which meant marriage vows. We did not want our relationship to boomerang later with a false sense of obligation.

So many times, as I counsel couples in mid-life who are having difficulties, I discover a surprising number of cases in which one or the other feels that he or she was forced into the marriage. When we get down to specifics, it turns out to have been premarital intercourse that resulted in a sense of "belonging" and therefore of obligation.

Some of the more modern students of sexual relationships might say, "Yes, and when we remove the cultural conditioning of obligation that goes along with intercourse, then we will be free to enjoy the relationship without hang-ups."

That seems fine in theory, if we can accept the possibility that intercourse has no inherent bonding characteristics. But suppose it *does?* Then no deculturization will ever remove the deep feeling of belonging two people have when they share such a powerful, beautiful experience. This feeling of belonging is exactly what the Scriptures teach, and what many cultures through the ages have taught. It is an almost universal human understanding.

But back to the concept of intimate communication in sexual relationships. In sexual intercourse, two persons completely bare themselves to one another—not only physically, but emotionally and personally in the deepest sense. In this act two persons "become one flesh"—and in the Hebrew understanding of the word, that was not just a fleshly or physical union but one involving the total personality. It was under the Greek influence that we thought we could divide the human personality into segments. True, facets of the personality are identifiable, but they are not separable. Each of us is an integrated whole, and one part of our personalities interacts constantly with the other parts; they never can function separately. Thus the psyche and covenant factors of our personalities are involved with the sexual. That is why, when a convenience relationship comes to an end, one or both persons feel they "have been had."

To put it another way, the total personality is like a plant, with sex the flower. Cut the flower from the stem and the roots, and it soon withers. Cut sex from the total relationship of life, and it cannot hold two persons together. In fact it becomes stale, even objectionable.

The plant of the total relationship is made up of the stem of covenant, the leaves of common commitments and basic agreements, the roots of spiritual commitment, and the soil of social and religious heritage. When the whole plant is strong, the blossoms of sexual joy actually multiply and become more exciting and fragrant with the years!

Memory and association also have a strong and invigorating influence on sexual activity. Couples who have planned and then joyfully "worked" for a child, always remember the sexual act as the one in which their gift of joy was conceived. As their child grows and matures, and becomes a creative, joyful person, the sexual relationship of the parents is wonderfully enhanced. The tough times, the periods of glad surprise, slogging through monotonous "deserts" and climbing awesome "peaks" all have a reference point of association, the single desire for a child and the joy of conception.

Sexual relationships do not always culminate in intercourse. At times, a quiet closeness between husband and wife can be of exquisite, relaxing refreshment. "Tactile tenderness," "cutaneous contact," or "Vitamin S [for *skin*]," when mixed with hours of sharing and conversation, can leave a couple refreshed and filled with a glowing sense of unity.

By all means, talk about sex before marriage. Your agreement or disagreement can make the difference between the experience of oneness or the agony of a division that grows wider with each passing year.

Children

"What are children?"

A foolish question? I don't think so. It is a very basic question. Is a child a social responsibility? If so, he might get the feeling that the sooner he is gotten out of the way, the better—which isn't the best way to make a child feel that his parents take a delight in him.

"Is our child an extension of our own ego?"

I certainly hope not. A child may have some characteristics of mother and father, but the child is a unique creation, a totally individual combination of strengths and weaknesses. He or she is not here to duplicate Aunt So and So or Grandfather Such and Such. Each child is a special creation for whom God has a plan, and the task of the parents is to help that child find out who he or she is without seriously tampering with the results.

Some of the first questions a couple ask are: "How many children should we have, if any? Are we only to replace ourselves, or disregard zero population growth?" I know one young couple who refuse to bring young humans into the maelstrom of hatred we call life on earth. "How do we feel about birth control, and by what methods? Under what circumstances, if any, would we agree upon abortion?"

"Would we consider children to be an inconvenience, and if so, when? Only in the early part of the marriage, or all through it? And what would be inconvenienced? Travel, career, personal freedom, social life?"

"What fears do we have regarding children? That we won't be up to the job of raising them? Childbirth? Genetic deformity? Financial incapability? Fear of world cataclysm?"

"Who is going to raise the children? Is that the wife's job, or does the father get into the act also? If he does, how and with what responsibilities?"

"What will be our standards of discipline? Will we stand together, or will the little rascal be able to get a wedge in between us? If we disagree on a given matter of discipline, how will we handle it?"

"Is the dinner table a good place for discipline?"

"Can I tell the children, 'When Daddy comes home, you are going to get a spanking?' Or do we operate on the basis of whoever sees the misbehavior administers the discipline?"

Perhaps one of the most important questions is, "Who is more important—my spouse or the children?"

I hope it will be the spouse. After all, your spouse is the one you will live with before the children come and after the children are gone. Moreover, if children sense that they can drive a wedge between their parents, believe me, the plans are already being made! But when a child senses that Mom and Dad are together and unshakable, he may have moments of frustration because he can't work one against the other, yet that very frustration will turn into a sense of security and

certainty—"If I can't drive them apart, nothin' can."
Both the child's feet stand on a unified foundation. If
Mom and Dad can be separated, then the child stands
on a foundation that is shifting beneath his feet. No
wonder his little face fills with panic—"If *I* can tear
them apart, what else can?" That insecurity and uncer-
tainty will affect the remainder of his life.

And one last question might be, "What gifts does
each of us bring to the rearing of our children?" Above
all, I hope your little one will feel that he is a delight to
you both. Nothing will prepare him for life better than
knowing he makes people happy!

We had gone over to the Taylors' home one evening
for dinner. They were the kind of folks who were a joy
to be around—no airs, and ample love for everybody,
including their little son Josh. Most of the early evening
Josh roamed around the room, checking in on each
guest and getting love from different ones. Then the
baby-sitter took him upstairs, got him ready for bed,
and allowed him to come down one last time to say
goodnight to everyone. He toddled around in his "Doctor Dentons," giving everybody a kiss and a hug. Then
his daddy gave him a loving pat on his bottom, and he
headed toward the stairs. I couldn't help calling after
him, "Good-night, Josh—we love you!"

He kept right on going, concentrating on lifting his
stubby little legs over those big stairs, but he called
right back, "I love me too!"

What a great way for a child to feel! Knowing his

family, I was sure they had probably made him feel that way from the moment he was born. And having received, he is going to be able to give!

Finances

"What is money?"

Every couple should know. And yet, sometimes it goes so fast we might answer that question by half jesting and half crying, "I wish I knew! I'd like to see some!"

In all seriousness, we need to ask the question, and we need to arrive at an operational agreement.

"Is money our *summum bonum*—our highest goal?"

"Is money our basis of security?"

Or, turn the question around, "What will we do for money, and what will we *not* do for money?"

"What will we not give up for money?"

"What is the importance of money and physical possessions in our marriage? Money means *something* to all couples; what does it mean to us?"

Many couples are confronted with a dilemma by Christ's words: "No one can serve two masters; for either he will hate the one and love the other, or he will be devoted to the one and despise the other. You cannot serve God and mammon [materialism]" (Matthew 6:24 RSV). For those who choose to serve the god of mammon, religion—which can outwardly appear to be so important and staunchly defended—becomes only a cloak or veneer. It is never allowed to influence the outcome of the money game. And certainly, for these folks, it would be unthinkable for religion to encounter or challenge the economic system.

During the days of the open housing controversy, I had preached on several occasions on the theme of our oneness in Christ, and therefore the oneness we had in communal relations. Subsequently, a black family enrolled their child in the Sunday school. After one of the services, I heard a commotion in the courtyard and stepping toward the action, was suddenly confronted by a man who saw me and bolted from the crowd. As he approached, he deliberately reached into his back pocket, pulled out his wallet, and waved it under my nose—not a half-inch away. He was a vocal Christian, highly successful in his business and living in a sumptuous house in one of the finest sections of the city. With irate intensity, he fairly shouted, "Louis Evans, I like you, but if what you do in this church lowers my property value by one dime, I'll fight you up and down the streets!" Apparently, I had threatened his god.

Money is a symbol of life, for it represents our labor and our creative individuality. Money, and the manner in which we use it, communicate a great deal about our personalities. Money is one of the principal ways we express our loyalties and priorities, so that when Christ calls for us to tithe, he very quickly gets a response, one way or the other! How important is God in your giving?

Actually, all Christians should tithe, right off the top of their income. That should be the first check written each month. This is simply a recognition that God is Lord of all of life. The "earth is the Lord's" and we are but using it for a while. If, as a people, we misuse it, the Lord will sooner or later give it to others.

Recently a rather antagonistic middle-aged church member challenged me to give him one good reason why he should tithe. I gave him several, beginning with the one above and going on to mention the fact that a Christian is one who considers himself a manager or steward—for Christ. In his death upon the cross, Christ paid a price for our liberation, and in his Resurrection he gave us the power for new life—something for which we should be deeply grateful, *if* we understand and have experienced what Christ has done for us.

Then suddenly an idea came over me. I shot his question back to him, slightly altered: "Give one good reason why you should *not* tithe!" He gave me several, none of them very good. But they told me who his master was, and it was not Christ. It was mammon. His cloak of religiosity had been blown aside and it allowed me to see his real uniform underneath.

That same kind of antagonism can erupt in a marriage when a couple do not agree on financial priorities. So, before your marriage—or even after it—it's a good idea to set aside some quiet time and acquaint each other with your feelings about money. For instance, who is going to be the "money bags?" I hope that, although you are conscious of each other's gifts regarding financial management, both of you will accept some of the responsibility for these duties. If not, the "manager" gets all the flak when something goes wrong. Both of you should be in on the budget making and decisions, although each should have some part of the budget he or she administers without constant referral to the other. Moreover, each should have some "mad money" to spend for *anything* desired.

And, please, don't get in so deep that you can't see your way out, or that the light at the end of the tunnel will be so far away you won't be able to see it. Life is too short to spend it at each other's throats, which is where most couples seem to fly when things get tight financially. Money problems stand right near the top of the list as causes for sunken marriages.

Early in our marriage, Colleen and I were always bumping our noses into financial dead ends. Either we had an insurance bill to pay or an unexpected repair bill, or Christmas or vacation would leave us devastated, and me on the verge of panic. "Why punish ourselves this way?" we finally said. "We know we will have to spend those amounts, so why not get ready for them?"

Difficult though it was, we began to lay aside the monies in an accrual account. We added up all the big payments that came due each year, divided the sum by twelve, and had the bank take that amount out of our checking account each month and put it into a saving account. Then, when a bill came due, we simply withdrew the proper amount, put it into our checking account, and paid the bill. We even went out to dinner on the interest on that account! What a relief! Now, true, we're in a slight pinch every month, but it surely beats the panic and the strain on our relationship. We found that instead of paying somebody else 8 to 10 percent for credit, we could pay ourselves 6 percent by saving our money. Put those together and you have a 14 to 16 percent difference, which is not small change!

One of the great joys of managing our money has been "dreaming." Right now we have hopes of building a little vacation cabin with our own hands somewhere in the "high country," and all the family is in on it. During our last vacation period, son Dan was working on some preliminary drawings, Andie was talking to a couple of her friends who think they want to help us build, and Tim and Jim were gathering tools. Now, we don't know when our chance will come, but we are putting money away for our dream. We're trying to "go lean" for it, and though the shocking expenses of the college years plague us, we find the dreaming is half the fun! The simplicity a couple achieve while striving toward a dream is one of the most unifying experiences a marriage can have.

"What is money?" A source of great joy when top priority is given to the Lord and the needs of the world —and the rest fulfills a dream with a purpose.

Friends

Several years ago, a lovely young woman came to Colleen and wept out her story of her husband's rudeness to her friends. He thought they were "uncouth" because they laughed openly, "uncultured" because they were not well heeled, and "sickeningly sweet" because they showed their love for one another with hugs and embraces.

"It hurts me so much," the woman sobbed. "It's not only that he rejects such neat people—he's also rejecting part of me! I've known and loved these people for years, and they are part of my life!"

She was right. Friends are a part of us, and in a marriage it is important for a husband and wife to accept each other's friends. That does not mean they must make them their best friends, but it does mean that they should honor their spouse's friendships and those needs his or her friends fulfill.

I have some flying friends, some golfing friends, and some buddies who work on cars with me. Colleen has friends with whom she can talk politics or with whom she shares concerns in the community or involvements such as the Hunger Task Force. We both give up some segment of time to the other for the development of these friendships.

Then there are those friends we both enjoy. No marriage is sufficient to itself. Each needs elements of an extended family, of persons who have covenanted to be available to us and sensitive to our needs. We call these friends our "warm fuzzies." We don't have to dress up or be "on duty" with them. We can relax in their presence—even snooze on their couch if we want to!

Sometimes, however, friendships can create problems in a marriage. "My best friend" can short-circuit the best-friend relationship that spouses should have with each other.

In the Song of Solomon there is a beautiful expression (which you must know we like!): "This is my beloved and this is my friend . . ." (5:16 RSV). When certain intimate concerns are hidden from one's mate and told to a friend, that indicates one partner's distrust of the other. A husband and wife should be "best friend" to the other—and yet neither can expect a spouse to be all that he or she needs in every segment of life. That puts a tremendous burden on a mate by demanding something he or she cannot give and therefore stimulates those uncomfortable, painful feelings of inadequacy that usually hound most of us anyway.

If one partner says, "I can't make it without you," that puts the other in a straitjacket. It prevents him or her from taking certain kinds of risks that are necessary for a fulfilled life. I'm not talking about foolhardy risks but about those involved with challenges to our creativity and development as a person. Now, true, husbands and wives need one another and should make themselves available for the other's needs. If, however, the other is so dependent that he or she cannot get along alone for a short period of time, then the "box" closes in and the prison term begins.

The best marriages are made up of two people who could make it on their own if they had to, who do not clutch at their mate as though he or she were a life preserver in a stormy sea.

Dependent, independent, and interdependent are three very different words. The dependent person rides on the back of another, sucks all strength from the other, and gives little or nothing back. The independent person marches through life proudly and alone, shunning the loving ministry of those around him. But there is a period in which the dependent person must be able to stand on his own—not aloof or isolated, but strong, able to manage the affairs of life without whimpering or whining, capable of stepping into the harness and pulling a portion of the load. This makes the person interdependent—someone who gives according to ability and graciously receives according to need, someone who builds up the gifts and abilities of others while receiving their resources at the same time. So it should be among the two "best friends" who come together in a marriage.

At this point the question arises: "How much time should we spend with our friends outside our marriage? What will we do for friendships, and what will we *not* give up for friendships?"

Some marriages become smothered when too many friends eat up too much social time. Colleen and I ran into this phenomenon while I was doing postgraduate work in Scotland. We were aliens in a foreign land, although the Scots were most cordial and warm. (Don't ever let anyone tell you the Scots are mean and dour. Frugal, yes, but they will give you their last ounce of sugar, and walk halfway up the street with you if you ask directions.) With about a hundred Americans doing graduate work, however, it was not surprising that our social calendar was soon overloaded!

Colleen was nursing our first child, Dan, at the time, and although he was the model baby (of course!) he would not be hurried with his feeding. One night we tried to hurry the whole process because we were planning to go out, and he felt the tension. Perhaps Colleen was putting a little something "extra" into the milk that night, but Dan put up a howl! I thought I heard the strain of an old gospel song in his rebellion, "I shall not be, I shall not be [hurried]!"

Colleen looked at me and shook her head slowly. "Honey, we're going too fast," she said. "If we aren't smart enough to see it, little Dan is. And besides, I want more quiet time with you and Dan."

I mused quietly for a moment while I continued tying my tie. The early weeks of Dan's infancy had been idyllic. I remembered the red glow of the coal fire as I stoked it to life; the sweet sounds of Dan's nursing; the quiet talks with Coke (for a while anyway; then, she claims, I slept through most of the feedings!). I recalled the serenity of sitting on the loveseat, Dan freshly bathed, powdered, and tucked into his soft pajamas, humping his little back in a slow rhythm, his head on my shoulder, as we talked and sang. Soon his little body moved more slowly. I could feel his breathing take on that steady pace, and finally his little hand dropped from my chest and was limp at his side—"He's cashed in his chips, honey."

We would tuck him into his crib, and go back to the den for a night of study or letter writing until BBC's third program would sign off with those familiar words, "Goodnight, goodnight all, goodnight."

We had time to be, to live, to share, to think clearly, to pray on those nights. We emerged from the nursery blinking but mellow and very much together. Now the hectic pace, so typical of our beloved homeland, started to accelerate, but it was increasingly an unacceptable way of life. The answer was evident. We had to put time aside for ourselves. Our social life was threatening our marriage with its tyranny, and it was time for us to declare our independence from it. With Dan's help, we did.

Home

When a couple discuss the kind of home they would like to have when they are married, there are two important things to remember: (1) They shouldn't let the home run them, and (2) neither should they run away from their home. *Home is the basic building block of*

a society. Home is the place where we interact in such
a way that our personalities are shaped and we emerge
as individuals. Here we find security. Home contains
the necessary elements that help us to live as human
beings. Therefore it has to be given a high priority
within our whole pattern of life. We cannot allow our
careers, our professional and educational interests, our
social or community obligations to keep us out of touch
with our home. If we do, we will not have the energy,
the confidence, or the resources to carry out those
other commitments.

A home runs us when we put too much emphasis on
its size, location, expenses, and furnishings. I suppose
most couples, at one time or another, take on too much
of a house, as we did, and find that it runs them instead
of the other way around. Years ago we got a terrific buy
—a large, beautiful house with a spacious yard for a
very low price. But keeping it up was something else.
It took Dan and Tim three hours to cut the grass, and
they were at the age where they had more interesting
things to do. Then we had to put in shrubs and trees,
which not only were expensive, but had to be cut and
trimmed regularly. We didn't have nearly enough fur-
niture for so much interior space, nor could we afford
to go out and buy more. Our car was getting old, and
we couldn't afford to replace it because every penny
was going into the house.

I was on everyone's back—because the house was on
my back! And not just financially, although—as Coke

pointed out in chapter 1, that, too, was a disaster. Beautiful as it was, we finally decided, "Who needs it?" We sold it and bought a much smaller house with a charming but maintainable little piece of land. In fact, one summer we vacationed at home and added on to that little house, with all the family involved in the framing, shingling, plastering, painting, and decorating. We had been short a bathroom, because with four teenagers one and a half baths didn't seem to suffice. So Mom and Dad were to have their own. And what a bath! We designed a room with a sunken tub and a large plate glass window looking out into a private garden in which we planted azaleas, a small palm tree, and bedding plants. Double sinks and dressing areas were included for convenience, and I must admit it was a touch of the lovely! And when that bath was all finished, *everybody* used it!

Even now, the children look back on that vacation as a very special time, one they are eager to repeat. Next time round, Andie wants to learn more about the plumbing!

Even Grandma and Grandad Evans got up on the scaffold and helped shingle the roof—to the consternation or admiration of the passersby on the street, some of whom recognized Dad. Seeing such an imposing figure in overalls that stood up by themselves from all the paint and boat varnish they had accumulated through the years was more than some could believe. But to us it was a hilarious adventure. We all had dedicated a major portion of our summer to our home; we had made it a priority, and that was worth it!

A couple should also agree on how their home will be used. Is it for family only, a place secluded from the world, or is it open to others?

I was brought up to think of the home as a place where people were to be made welcome. I'm glad Colleen was able to agree with that, or we could have had a conflict. In our first apartment at the seminary, we spent our first Thanksgiving as husband and wife. "How about inviting a couple of the seminarians who don't have families?" Colleen suggested. I concurred, and before we knew it the list had grown to eight. We borrowed a table from the seminary, some folding chairs, filled the tiny front-room study with happy students and even a visiting professor who has remained one of our dearest friends. And that set the mold. Thereafter our house always seemed to be the place for large gatherings.

One night recently our son Jim recalled his happy memories of our Bel Air living room filled with charter members of the new church—all of them singing, studying, laughing, and praying together. At times the laughter was so enticing that the children would crawl out into the hall where they could hear but not be seen, and they fell fast asleep on the floor. Guests going out would call our attention to the fact that there were four little bodies in the hall and would help us put them back into bed.

In some cases a family comes and goes without any sort of coordinated schedule or agreement regarding the time they spend together. Each person is off in a different direction according to his or her own timetable. "I'm tired of serving dinner three or four times a night," one mother complained. "But what can I do? I can't let my kids live on snacks."

Here is one place where I would stand and fight—someone needs to take the initiative in getting the family to set aside the dinner hour for family time. If not, the camel of the world will take up all the room in the tent. Dad will let business eat him up, Mother will be too busy with her work or social groups, the children's homework or extracurricular activities will run right through the dinner hour, education will eat up weekends, holidays, and vacations. There will be no time left for the family to sit down together and share their experiences, their plans, their pains, hopes, or problems. Gradually, invisible barriers will begin to separate them, and soon they will feel like strangers in one another's presence. Should any outside force so threaten a family, the whole country would be up in arms, yet we often give up by default what we would give our lives to defend.

I am glad Colleen puts her foot down about dinner time. If too many "emergencies" keep me from those moments with my family, I hear about it! And rightly so.

Goals

If someone were to ask you, "Do you have a good marriage?" and you were to answer, "Yes, I surely do!" by what criteria would you judge your marriage to be a success? Included among the most popular responses I receive is "being happy."

At first glance, that seems reasonable enough. But I have learned that if happiness is seen as a goal of marriage, rather than as a by-product of other factors, a couple become increasingly incapable of dealing with unhappy or difficult circumstances. Instead of meeting problems head-on, they look for escape routes, denying themselves those lasting victories and discoveries of strength that come from leaping into the arena of life and honestly struggling with the issues. But who is going to struggle with *un*happiness if happiness is the goal? Such a relationship degenerates into shallow pleasure seeking, leaving behind a trail of unresolved debris that eventually overwhelms one or both partners.

We cannot seek happiness for its own sake. Happiness is the product of clear agreements, honest struggles, creative cooperation. Happiness is two people striding together through the routines of life's flatlands, slogging through some deep valleys, and climbing laboriously to mountaintops whose vistas make all the trekking worthwhile. The greatest joys come after some of the most difficult struggles.

Some couples tell me that one of their goals is to grow together, to help one another become all that he or she can be.

There are few things more satisfying than to see one we love reaching his full potential. To hold another up on hands of prayer, to support her with all the resources we can muster, to watch her touch the stars of her dreams, sends a thrill of delight through a lover's heart.

Many couples have as their goal a high position in a corporation, and everything is sacrificed to that. Some want to be included in the highest echelons of society, whereas others strive for political positions in their community, state, or nation. Great ambitions can consume a family's time and energy to the point where each member becomes starved for personal attention. The "best" schools and "anything you want" are poor substitutes for the presence, concern, and support of a family member.

Some couples tell me their goal is to live for Christ. They want to do all they can to build his Kingdom, to work with young people or the aged, spending great amounts of energy, time, or money to make the church strong and effective.

What a vast variety of goals there are and how radically they differ! At times they come into conflict with one another. Suppose that opposition and radical difference were present within a marriage? Tragically two people often come together in the excitement of romance and infatuation and never bother to talk over these things. How many of us have pulled back the curtain of our lives and showed each other the script that controls our "play" and all the "props" that will be used? Have we published what we honestly would like as our "agenda" for the other to read? If so, and if these goals agree, then two persons have a good chance of experiencing a glorious companionship that gets better with time.

Remember, all God's relationships are designed to operate on the law of increasing returns; they improve with age! At times we will ask ourselves if we can contain the happiness and joy. The answer is "No!" It will simply have to spill over onto others.

Blessed is the couple whose God is the Lord, who said, "These things have I spoken to you, that my joy may be in you, and that your joy may be full" (John 15:11 RSV). "I came that you might have life and have it abundantly" (*see* John 10:10).

6

My Best Friend

TWO COUPLES . . . two loving, lovable couples . . . so similar and yet so different. Two marriages . . . one that seems to thrive on challenges and one that was shattered by them.

Evan and Sara are two people I like very much. When I am with Sara, she tells me all about her husband, Evan, and the wonderful research he is doing in the area of world hunger. Evan talks more about Sara's work as a publicist than he does about his own. They have three beautiful children, all grown up and starting families of their own. The amazing thing about Sara and Evan is that they are often separated by their work and have been for much of their long marriage. But I have the feeling that they are very good friends as well as loving husband and wife.

Phil and Yvonne are extremely likable, too—but when I think about them I am filled with sadness. At first they were so happy. They went everywhere together—all around the world, in fact, because Phil's business required him to travel for long periods of time.

When their three children were small, Phil and Yvonne
took them along on their trips . . . until it was time for
them to enter school. Taking them out of one school
and putting them into another just wasn't good for the
children, so Yvonne decided that it was time their family had a home. She and Phil bought a house, and
Yvonne remained there with the children while Phil
traveled.

But Phil was gone for long periods of time whenever
he went away, which meant that Yvonne had to do a lot
of things she wouldn't have done if he had been home.
She had to make most of the family decisions. If anything went wrong with the house, it was up to her to
have it repaired. When the children had problems, she
solved them by herself. By the time Phil came home
between trips, she was a different, far more independent person than she had been . . . and somehow he too
had changed. Living for so long in another part of the
world, he had established new roots and made new
acquaintances—all of whom were unfamiliar to
Yvonne. Being away from the children for so long, he
couldn't relate to them. He was concerned and affec-
tionate—because he loved them very much—but they
couldn't get close to each other. Neither could he and
Yvonne. Finally they got a divorce.

Separations break up a lot of marriages, yet there
obviously was a difference between these two couples.
Something held one marriage together in spite of the
separations.

I think we can't overlook the fact that some separations are simply too long. Evan was never away for more than two weeks at a time, whereas with Phil it was a matter of months.

But there was something else. There was a home . . . Evan and Sara's marriage has always had a home to embrace it. It is a specific place, a unique and nourishing environment in which both of them can meet—by letter, or telephone, or even in their imaginations—when they are apart. By the time Phil and Yvonne had a home, it was too late. Home was nothing more than a geographical location.

When Louie is away, he can visualize the children and me in our home. It's almost a form of communication with us.

Evan and Sara also have a common faith in a common goal. She believes in the importance of his work, and so she can make sacrifices for it. That's the way I feel about Louie's work . . . so, when he has to travel, which he frequently does, I may not like it, but I accept the need for it. In fact, I feel as if I'm a part of it. A friend of mine, who has a remarkably good marriage in spite of many necessary separations, says, "I'd rather be with the right man *some* of the time than the wrong man all of the time." I feel that way, too.

Yvonne couldn't feel that way about Phil's work. His goal was success—and unfortunately that just wasn't enough to compensate for his absence. And when important matters came up . . . when the children had problems or when Yvonne needed to talk something out with a friend, Phil couldn't be there. His work had to come first.

The big difference in these two marriages—I think—is that Evan and Sara are able to handle their separations because they are friends as well as marriage partners. Yes . . . and a friend is someone who is there when you need him. Evan and Sara want to be together, they have a happy, stable marriage, and they are together enough to sustain their relationship. They know they can count on each other—because each comes first in the other's life.

I believe in the kind of marriage that allows each partner enough space to develop and be himself. And would you believe it?—that idea isn't new! . . . I like what William Penn had to say about it:

> There is no Friendship where there is no Freedom. Friendship loves a free Air, and will not be penned up in straight and narrow Enclosures. I will speak freely, and act so too; and take nothing ill where no ill is meant; nay, where it is, 'twill easily forgive, and forget too, upon small Acknowledgements.

But I also believe in a sense of belonging . . . and when we belong to someone, we owe that person something. We owe him or her first claim to our time, and we owe him or her our fidelity.

I think it's good for both partners to have interests

they enjoy pursuing on their own, but if those interests take up the better part of their free time, then they've got problems. Most couples we know don't have much discretionary time, and if they were to spend most of it doing other things with other people, they would almost never be together.

I wouldn't want to spend *too* much time doing my own thing, either. I would rather try to learn to like some of the things my husband enjoys doing . . . and I'd like to share some of my pleasures with him. For instance, ordinarily I'd never think of taking up flying— I'm a white-knuckle flyer!—but because Louie loves it, and because I want to be with him more of the time, I'm learning to like it . . . at least enough to be part of some pretty special little jaunts. He does the same for me. I love to see a good play, but I'm usually the one who has to get theater tickets because that just isn't Louie's thing. Still, he does enjoy a play once we get there, and it enriches our life. Yes, it's wonderful for each partner to give the other a little space of his or her own . . . but not so much that they can't be together. As friends, they should be able to submit to each other's tastes and interests.

It's good for a couple to be able to function independently of each other. But alienation is something else. When two people are independent—or better still, *inter*dependent—they have their own identities and they communicate their needs to each other. Alienated people don't communicate at all. Each is totally involved in his own world—by choice or because he feels cut off from the other person's world.

Careers aren't the only things that can cause separation. Evan and Sara have a very close marriage even though they both have careers. But I have talked with some couples who are always available to each other, and yet their marriages are coming apart. They have hidden resentments toward each other, and that in itself can be an endless separation.

It's a matter of attitude. If a husband and wife have a real friendship as part of their marriage, then they can handle the times apart like two good friends who have not seen each other for a while. Once they get back together, it's as if they never had been separated.

"And the Lord God said, 'It is not good for man to be alone . . .' "—and so we were created male and female for companionship. God intended friendship as part of marriage. It is hoped that, in addition to the attraction they feel for each other, two people will make a lifelong commitment because there is also a deep friendship between them. That friendship will serve them well, because children are not a part of all marriages . . . and even when there are children, they come and they go, so that eventually a couple find themselves alone again.

Children can be a great joy, but they were never meant to sustain a marriage. In day-to-day living—in the world of prickly beards, hair in rollers, bouts of illness, and cases of the grumps, as well as the fun and delight of building a home together—perhaps the thing that will matter most is that two people are real and trusting friends.

If a man and a woman are friends before they marry —and if their friendship matures during their marriage —then there will be no "twenty-year fracture" when their children begin leaving home. . . . Rather, they will find that at last they have the time they have always wanted for each other.

And what is a friend? Many things. . . .

A friend is someone you are comfortable with, someone whose company you prefer. A friend is someone you can count on—not only for support, but for honesty.

A friend is one who believes in you . . . someone with whom you can share your dreams. In fact, a real friend is a person you want to share all of life with—and the sharing doubles the fun.

When you are hurting and you can share your struggle with a friend, it eases the pain. A friend offers you safety and trust . . . whatever you say will never be used against you.

A friend will laugh with you, but not at you . . . a friend is fun.

A friend will pray with you . . . and for you.

My friend is someone with whom I can share my ideas and philosophies, someone with whom I can grow intellectually. If one marriage partner is growing intellectually and the other is not, then their relationship will be strained. So it's good for a couple to read and discuss the same kinds of literary, political, social, and religious material. They ought to be aware of what is going on in their community, their nation, and their world. This is one of the ways in which they shape their goals. Since friends are people who have common goals, growing together intellectually is a form of friendship.

My friend is one who hears my cry of pain, who senses my struggle, who shares my lows as well as my highs.

When I am troubled, my friend stands not only by my side, but also stands apart, looking at me with some objectivity. My friend does not always say I am right, because sometimes I am not.

One of the worst things that can happen in a marriage is for one partner to take the side of the other when that side is invalid. If a wife is having difficulties in her relationship with her boss, she is not helped by a husband who reacts by saying, "Why, that dirty so-and-so!" Immediately the issue becomes clouded with emotion. The wife seeks more support for her stand from her other friends and co-workers, and finally the issue becomes so polarized that it cannot be resolved.

My friend does not do that. When my stand is invalid, my friend may say, "Maybe your attitude is a bit defensive."

Now, when my friend does this, I must admit that it's not the happiest time in our relationship. Part of me would rather have him in my corner, whether I'm right or wrong—but another part of me says, "Wait a minute —you know his point is well taken. You did miss some clues. If you continue in your former thinking, you and the others with you are going to get hurt. So don't be proud."

Honesty has to be part of friendship. Sometimes it disrupts the calmness of a marriage, but it pays off in the long run. When my friend challenges my point of view, it helps me to get in touch with my feelings. It also forces me to become more objective about myself.

This is a delicate balancing act in a marriage relationship. If one partner assumes the role of critic, then he's blown it. But if he can stand a bit apart and at the same time let his partner know that he is loyal, then friendship becomes an art form.

A friend is not primarily a critic. At least, not *my* friend. I know he loves me. And when he stimulates me to think more clearly, he adds strength to our relationship—and to me. If I find that I have to change my way of thinking, then I am free to do it in the privacy of my own counsel. In the presence of my friend, I haven't lost, nor am I ridiculed.

My lover, my friend—this is what a marriage partner should be.

There are other friends in my life, and I value them highly. But only my best friend knows me so intimately. More than anyone else, he recognizes my strengths and accepts my weaknesses with patience. Only he is sensitive to all my moods and vulnerabilities. It is with him that I can become one.

Through him—my husband, my friend—Christ's love comes most powerfully into my life. Some of my deepest needs are voiced in moments of prayer with him. I give thanks to God most earnestly with him—and for him.

7

Keeping Romance Alive

IT WAS A BLUSTERY, cold day in Washington. It was also our day off, and a good time to indulge in one of our favorite treats—an afternoon at the theater. As it turned out, *A Matter of Gravity* was not my choice for the Play of the Year, but Katherine Hepburn made it well worth the price of admission! She was magnificent! As we walked away from the theater in the early evening, I turned on my mind's "instant replay" where I could hear Miss Hepburn deliver certain key lines and relive the delight of her inimitable delivery.

One line in particular kept coming back again and again. Miss Hepburn was portraying an elderly widow playing hostess to her grandson and his friends, and at one point she was queried by one of the guests about the quality of her marriage. She replied, with great dignity, "It was a triumph! But it took *some* doing."

As she spoke the words, a couple who are close friends and were sitting a few rows ahead of us wheeled around to make sure we had grasped that line. And Louie, sitting next to me, gave me an elbow in the ribs.

Apparently it was a line with special meaning for all of us, not just for me. For marriage *is* a triumph—at least it *can* be . . . but, as Miss Hepburn eloquently reminded us, "It takes *some* doing."

Perhaps no aspect of marriage takes more "doing" than that of keeping romance alive. Romance takes time, energy, planning, and creativity—yes, it's work! But, like seeing Katherine Hepburn in a play, the delightful results make it well worth the price you pay.

Recently I read a best-selling book in which the writer suggested that wives ought to greet their husbands at the door at the end of the day dressed in a baby-doll nightie and high heels. Well, I could hardly wait! When Louie came home that night I—no, I didn't. But what I did do was ask him how he'd *feel* if I greeted him that way one night, and he replied, "I'd like the implication, but not the getup."

Then he chuckled. "That sure would be out of character for us! But I could accept a variety of expressions that say 'I want time with you.' The thing that turns me on is not what you're wearing—it's you as a person . . . knowing that you desire me . . . that we desire each other."

Then, after a pause, he added, "Come to think of it, that getup might be just the ticket for some people."

And he's right! If a nightie and high heels work for the woman who wrote that book—and apparently it does—that's great! But it wouldn't be natural for us. There are no rules for keeping romance alive that will work in the same way for everyone. But one thing that romance does require is a periodic planned sharing we might call "quality time" . . . time for two people to be together in a very private way, doing whatever pleases *them*.

When our children were small, we played a little game for two called "Make a Tunnel." All we did was to cup our hands around our eyes and bring our heads together until our hands touched, forming a tunnel between us. Then we simply looked into one another's eyes, and with everything around us temporarily blocked out of mind and view, we "let the rest of the world go by." The game didn't take much time—just long enough to look deep and feel something warm and satisfying inside. Today I asked Andie, our nineteen-year-old daughter, what "making a tunnel" meant to her way back then, and she said, "It made me feel secure, warm, close, and very special." I thought to myself, that's what *romance* in a marriage makes you feel—secure, special, and close. So perhaps "quality time"—looking deep into the eyes of the one you love and "making a tunnel" in whatever way pleases you both—is essential to keeping romance alive.

Recently I was talking to a friend whose husband died a year ago, just before his fiftieth birthday. They had known a good marriage, and she misses him and their life together terribly. As we talked, my friend's eyes filled with tears. I don't think I'll ever forget what she said: "He saw me in a way no one else ever had. And now that the one who thought I was *most* special, *most* beautiful, *most* unique, is gone, I just don't feel I'm as much those things anymore." She was not complaining —she told me she was rich in memories now because theirs had been a great love, a romance to the end. Obviously, they had taken time to look deep, to see in each other what no one else could see, and to feel warm and secure in their love. However a couple achieves it, this is "quality time."

We know several couples who seem to be especially successful at keeping the glow glowing. Each couple has their own interpretation of quality time, depending on their personalities and life-style.

Dee and Bill Brehm, for instance, from whom we borrowed the term "quality time," are extremely busy people. Bill is presently the Assistant Secretary of Defense, for legislative affairs. Dee is a fine French cook who gives cooking lessons in her home; she also is active in the covenant group ministry of the church and gives parties (seven-course dinners!) for half the world as it passes through Washington. But in spite of their full schedules, Dee and Bill give Christ, their marriage, and their family highest priority. Each Wednesday night, barring a national crisis, they have their "quality time." Dee prepares one of their favorite French meals, sets a beautiful, candlelit table in their bedroom, and when Bill comes home they close the door. Wednesday night is theirs—no children, no phone calls (except emergencies), and no interruptions. What they do after dinner

—well, who knows? Whatever it is, it nurtures them and their relationship—and it shows.

Another couple we love and admire greatly are Mary Jane and John Dellenback. Somehow I always think of them as a team—the way they pull together, honoring one another's interests, has given their marriage a deep sense of oneness and romance.

"A big part of the excitement in our relationship comes from our support of each other," Mary Jane says. "John has encouraged me to become part of his professional life. Traveling with him, now, as director of the Peace Corps, and watching the empathetic way he deals with people—the impressive way he dispatches problems—gives me a tremendous surge of pride. He says I've helped him become more skilled in dealing with people, and he has helped me become a more organized, careful thinker. He is the one who urged me to return to school and finish my degree. And he's proud of my accomplishment! My field of interest isn't his, but he listens and learns something of what is exciting me intellectually at the time."

Then Mary Jane remembered something and laughed. "Yes—and he was quick to point out, when we discussed this subject, that we aren't all *that* intellectual in our interest in each other! We just plain, physically, like to be together. We enjoy traveling together, playing tennis together, visiting museums together. We have a lot of fun."

Gene and Jeanine Arnold are another couple alive to

one another! Married since she was eighteen and he was nineteen, they have just celebrated their twenty-fifth anniversary, and they still become radiant in each other's presence.

"It's not that we never fuss," Jeanine says. "We fuss fast and get over it fast, and the experience cleanses us of petty grievances. Then we're free to give ourselves wholeheartedly again."

These two have many gifts in their marriage, but there is a special one that Louie and I call the gift of "anointing."

In the New Testament there is a touching scene in which Mary Magdalene anoints Jesus' feet with expensive ointment. Her gesture was more than a generous expression—it was downright extravagant—and the disciples reacted as many of us would to such an act. They reprimanded her, saying, "Why, that nard could have been sold for two hundred denarii and given to the poor."

But, as Mary threw practicality to the winds in a bold expression of affection, Jesus affirmed her! His response set an example, and through the centuries it became a custom to "anoint" a loved one with a costly gift. It is something many of us cannot do often . . . yet when it is done sincerely, rather than as a sad effort to buy someone's love, it can be a real boon to romance. Our friends, Gene and Jeanine, have learned to anoint one another with exactly that result.

Early in their marriage, Gene was a young Marine

and was sent to Korea. (Jeanine was pregnant when he left, and their baby, Jennifer, was four months old by the time he returned.) On Gene's small sergeant's salary things were tight financially . . . yet every month, on the date of their marriage, flowers arrived at their home back in the States. The bouquets became a tender link of two hearts whose marriage was also new and tender. Of course, they couldn't afford it, but the "anointing" bonded their relationship with thoughtful bursts of affection that continue to this day.

It is difficult for me to describe where Louie and I are in respect to keeping our romance alive. In fact, this chapter has been hard to write because I've become painfully, yet gratefully, aware of how good God has been to us in our relationship, and how little we sometimes give him to work with. True, we keep our Thursday nights for each other, but sometimes we are just too tired to do anything but go to bed . . . a respite for us both, certainly, but not always "quality time." There are pressures and crises in the ministry—even on Thursdays—and we sometimes lose our one night a week altogether. I remember one period in our last church when emergencies came in unrelenting waves. It was an incredible time of tragic teenage deaths, community trauma, with the church involved—as it should be—at the very core. After many weeks of little rest and no time alone together, the strain took a toll on our relationship. When the calm finally came, as it always eventually does, I called Louie's secretary and asked her to put me down on his schedule for lunch the first day he had a free noon hour. She wrote "Business Lunch" in his appointment book and then added the address of one of our favorite restaurants.

I still remember the look of surprise on Louie's face as he walked into the restaurant that day and found me waiting at a table for two. It was a very special time— Louie was tender, I shed a few tears, and, fortunately, the restaurant was not very crowded. It was a time of getting back in step, of agreeing to resist the pressures that could keep us apart.

Perhaps, though, it is right for us to yield to these pressures and needs of others occasionally—even if it means missing those special times of recreation together. Yet when we do, it is also right—and also necessary—to set up another "business lunch," or a dinner or a weekend out of town so that we can be tender and weepy, or whatever we must be in order to feel that we are walking hand in hand again. I guess what I'm saying is, we *are* committed to the need for "quality time" together, but we don't seem to be able to adhere to it rigidly. We get it—somehow—someway—because we need it—and even more significant, we *want* it.

Neither are we anointers, like Gene and Jeanine. Our "gifts" have been affirming notes pinned on pillows or left on desks . . . flowers, not from the florist, but picked by Louie along the road as he jogs in the morning. When it comes to costly gifts, we are both very practical. We always seem to be saving for some purpose or project. . . . So, when birthdays or anniversaries come along, our gift is usually a reminder to one another that we are "saving up." (With three of our four children in college, I don't need to tell you what we are "saving up" for!)

What works for one couple will not automatically work for another. Like so many parts of marriage, romance must be custom-made. And yet, in spite of the things we haven't done, God has blessed us with a love that is alive . . . with a romance that keeps us feeling special to each other.

When I asked Louie what was to him the most romantic thing we did together, without hesitation he said, "Backpacking in the high country." Now, bear in mind, we are at our grubbiest at that time . . . no perfume, candlelight, or soft music . . . but there *is* a feeling of partnership, a working together, a sharing of both the hardships and the exquisite beauty of the experience, and a stillness that is most romantic to both of us.

One of our special friends in California hates any kind of camping, and I can just hear her saying, "Well, my dear, to each his own." How true!

Romance is not made of shivers and tingles—in spite of what the movies may tell us! Romance is not even what we do—or don't do. Doing the right things may enhance romance, but basically romance is an attitude. It is a man and woman being alive to one another—not taking one another for granted. It is an atmosphere— a look that speaks more eloquently than words, a squeeze of the hand as you pass each other in a crowded room, a pat on the head or the shoulder for no particular reason. Romance is an element of fascination and delight that culminates in a deep desire to experience all of life with the one we love.

Romance helps make marriage the triumph it can be . . . a triumph that is both a gift from God, and one that "takes *some* doing."

8

Sex Is Something Special

I LET MYSELF in for a lot of teasing the other day when I said, "I love sex." I said it among good friends and in the context of a discussion about marriage, but because I didn't make myself quite clear, I've been teased a lot about my comment. But my friends knew what I meant. It was simply this: I love my husband, and sex is part of our marriage, and therefore I love sex.

Furthermore, I'm for emancipated sex. Now, I'm talking about sex within a lifelong commitment of marriage—sex that is enjoyed—thoroughly! I mean the kind of sex defined by Myron Brenton in *The American Male* as ". . . a free, spontaneous, primitive sexual response between men and women who look on each other as individuals rather than as walking stereotypes." By "primitive" I understand him to mean that we are free to be ourselves . . . free to enjoy. This is the kind of emancipated sex that is part of what makes marriage a growing adventure.

Our society seems to be obsessed with sex—and with sexual performance. It seems to me that sex is more enjoyable, more fun, more ministering when a couple can relax and enjoy it without being conscious of the rules and requirements of sexual fulfillment.

To put it simply, emancipated sex means—relax! Enjoy! And why not? For sex is good. If anyone has any doubts about it, the Bible has news for him.

No book speaks more honestly about sex than the Bible . . . and the Bible never states or even implies that sex is sin. In fact, we are told that God created sex, that he ordained it, and blessed it. Only when it is misused is it wrong. Sex between a man and woman who have made a lifelong commitment covenant with each other becomes what God intended it to be—a celebration of love and life.

The Scriptures tell us that sex is not something we "do" . . . sex is *part* of us. We are sexual beings with the ability to express our sexuality in different ways. This is not accident . . . each expression has a purpose.

The first purpose that comes to my mind is that of oneness. In Genesis 2:24 (RSV) we read: "Therefore a man leaves his father and mother and cleaves to his wife, and they become one flesh." For me, this command to be "one flesh" is as significant as the command "to be fruitful and multiply."

Today it's not uncommon to hear jokes about the Genesis account of woman being fashioned from a part of man. Yet in those verses there is something we can learn. For when a man and a woman first come together sexually in a covenant relationship, they share an almost mystical feeling that they are not coming together as two who have never known each other. Rather, there is the feeling that—somehow—from the beginning they have been part of each other and in their physical union they are completing each other. They are becoming one . . . again.

I like this sense of belonging in a marriage. . . . There are times, through the months and years, when a husband and wife share the same mountaintop experiences. Looking out over the same green meadows, the same meandering stream, they know that this is something they will never forget. It is theirs forever. They are so intensely aware of each other—physically, spiritually, and in the oneness of motive—that they are joined together with unbreakable bonds.

Oneness . . . how much a part of God's good purpose it is. Yet there are conditions to oneness. In the more traditional marriage services, a question is asked: Will you pledge your troth to. . . . ? As they answer "yes," the couple pledge themselves to enter into a *unique* relationship that promises, among other things, sexual fidelity.

In a Christian marriage faithfulness is expected of both husband and wife. Old-fashioned? Perhaps. Sensible? Definitely! Only when fidelity is their life-style can two people know the freedom and trust that enable them to express their love completely. In Proverbs, the writer warns us about the misuse of sexual life, and then goes on—in lovely, positive words of admonition—to faithfulness: "Drink water from your own cistern, flowing water from your own well. . . . Let your fountain be blessed, and rejoice in the wife of your youth . . ." (Proverbs 5:15–18 RSV). When two people are blessed with this kind of oneness and uniqueness in their marriage, it does not turn them inward toward their own private world. Quite the opposite . . . it seems to me they are more able to share their partners with life and other people, without jealousy or possessiveness, precisely because they *know* they have a holy, private place where they belong to each other. In this place they know the full and free expression of their love . . . it is there that they are refreshed and renewed, enabled to go out to other people and to the world. Not only they but all others are blessed by their faithfulness to the vows they made at the altar.

Sexual oneness can be achieved only by two people who feel they belong to each other in a larger sense, by two people who really care about each other as persons and are committed to sharing all of life. They must have a total relationship.

Of course, even within total completely faithful relationships, there are endless ways to stifle unity and oneness in sex and to sin against the spirit of our partner by a shabby attitude. If a husband or wife comes home from work, grunts some unintelligible greeting, eats without a word, and then hides behind the newspaper or a current best-seller until bedtime, he or she cannot expect a mate to turn into a passionate partner just because they get into bed together. Sex doesn't begin in the bedroom . . . *it permeates all of life,* and very often begins in the kitchen over orange juice and coffee. In our sexuality we express the quality of our everyday life, and when two people have lost touch with each other in the simple things, they may find themselves resisting intimacy because sex has no everyday love to express.

A very important part of oneness is submission. In fact, sexual unity calls for the *ultimate* in submission, as two people present themselves to each other, accepting each other just as they are. It is a test of trust, one that—in the beginning—requires courage for total unmasking of body and soul. For oneness means giving up the very private you. This kind of submission is not easy . . . for some it is much harder than for others . . . yet it is well worth the abandonment of self that it requires. Unless two people can surrender to each other, they will miss some of the glory of the oneness God has created for them.

One of the great purposes of sex is procreation: "And God blessed them, and God said to them, 'Be fruitful and multiply, and fill the earth and subdue it . . .' " (Genesis 1:28 RSV). The conception of a child is the most explicit way in which two people become one. And yet children are not to become an extension of a parental ego. Each child is a unique creation and has a particular destiny to fulfill. . . . He or she should never be expected to live out someone else's unfulfilled dreams.

As I think about sex for the purpose of procreation,
I am wondering about the aura in which the act of
conception takes place. In our society we take very
seriously the way in which a person dies. But the way
in which a person begins life is equally important. Are
the parents committed to each other? Are they com-
mitting themselves to the child? Is conception a fear?
—or a hope?

I also wonder, now that we are aware of the spiraling
rise in world population, of the many human beings
who die every day of malnutrition or hunger, if it isn't
time for us to exercise our procreative responsibility in
a new way. For generations we have done well at filling
the earth. . . . Perhaps now it is time for us to submit
to the *limits* of our earth. Of course, that's easy for me
to say, now that I've had the four children I've always
wanted. I can just hear our oldest son, who is our family
ecology and population expert, say, "Nice going, Mom.
How'd you manage that? Four kids in five years!" What
he means is, I'd have a hard time justifying myself if I
were having our children now—and he's right. Discovering the best way to exercise Christian responsibility
in this area is a task my generation has left to his.

Communication is another purpose of sex, and one
that is strongly supported in Scripture: "Now Adam
knew Eve his wife . . ." (Genesis 4:1 RSV).

The deepest human need is to be *known* and *loved*.
For most people the potential fulfillment of that need
is found in the close and covenanted relationship of

husband and wife. Communication—knowing and being known in depth—is one of the greatest joys of sex and of marriage itself. When a marriage has *soul,* and two people are growing together in their total relationship, there are moments of union that transcend both word and touch. Call it "mystical" if you wish . . . I call it "communicating." It is not an everyday occurrence, nor does it need to be. But once it happens, it leaves its mark not only on the marriage but on all of the couple's life.

The psychiatrist Abraham Maslow has found that, in self-actualizing people, love and sexual satisfactions improve with the age of the relationship. I love that! It confirms my belief—as does a book by Dr. Robert Butler, titled *Sex in the Sixties*—that all of God's relationships operate according to the law of increasing returns.

Of course, ill health and other unavoidable hindrances can get in the way for periods of time. Still, a couple who know oneness can feel optimistic about the effect of the passing years on their sexual life.

We know a couple who most certainly confirm this expectation. . . . Ken and Hilda were in their early sixties when we were in our twenties—and naturally we felt that sex was invented for people of our age. How wrong we were! One day Hilda took me aside and said, "Oh, Coke, since Ken has retired, we've having so much fun! We have time to do things we've wanted to do for years. We even go roller-skating! And our sex life!

—well, it's never been so good!" Isn't that wonderful! I gave Hilda a great big hug because I felt so happy for her—and for me, because she had expanded my limited idea of what happens to sex in the later years.

Ken and Hilda are in their eighties now, and the miles separate us from them. But the picture and message on their Christmas card each year assure us that life is still very capable of producing a large twinkle in their eyes!

If good sex is based on the fulfillment of each other's needs, then all the years a couple have lived together should increase their level of sensitivity to the things that please each other. Therefore, the communication that is part of sex should get better as time goes on.

When a man and woman marry, they *do* commit themselves to meet each other's needs. That is another purpose of sex made clear in the Scriptures. First Corinthians tells us that the husband does not own his body . . . his wife does. Conversely, the wife's body is not hers, but his (*see* 7:3–5).

People differ, marriages differ, and so, of course, do needs. There are great variations between couples when it comes to how intense, how frequent, how anything else their sexual expression should be. For these facets of sex there are no rules, no "must do" lists. Each couple must discover their own needs. But there are ways in which their concern for each other enables— even urges—them to minister to each other through their sexual relationship. Paul, in fact, says it is a "fraud" not to *minister* to each other in our sexual needs.

It seems to me that Christian husbands and wives especially owe it to one another to take their sexual relationship seriously. Well, on second thought, not *so* seriously that it can't be fun, but seriously enough to be really important and to merit undivided attention. Often when I think of the attitude surrounding sex, the verse "Whatsoever you do, do with all your heart" flashes across my mind. For what is more dismal than the thought of a halfhearted lover—a husband going through amorous motions while thinking of an upcoming sales meeting, or a wife planning the menu for a dinner party while giving her husband his "conjugal rights." A lot of the thrill and joy of sex begins right between the ears—in our mind, in our power of concentration, and in our ability to give ourselves to this God-given expression of love "with all our heart."

Of course, there are obstacles to this kind of wholehearted giving in sex . . . they come to everyone at times. We have mentioned illness, and then there is that archenemy of sex—fatigue. It is hoped these would last only a season and would be valid reasons, not masked excuses to avoid closeness. When someone uses these things as excuses and over a long period of time, there is real danger to the marriage . . . the person is asking for love and loyalty but at the same time closing the door to the closeness and the intimacy in which love and loyalty can grow.

Another obstacle to wholehearted giving is busyness.

Sex was not meant to be crowded into the tiny bits of time when a couple is least able to enjoy it. Of course, there will be those unexpected "brief encounters," but they should not become a steady diet. Sex cannot remain healthy and nourished while feeding continually from the crumbs off the table. When we are too busy to find time to express our love, we are *indeed* too busy!

Problems can also take a man and a woman away from each other sexually, and although sex is reconciling, it should not take the place of honestly and openly facing our problems. Sex is not an *escape* . . . it releases tension, and that is a *good* gift, but it is meant to set us up for life, not to take us from it.

The last purpose of sex I see stressed in Scripture is the golden thread of joy and pleasure that runs through every other purpose. Yet it is worthy and beautiful in itself. Once again, no two couples are alike, and there are no rules as to how each is to find pleasure. Whatever brings two people joy and a sense of well-being is right for them . . . and when these are affirmed again and again as they are when the couple are together sexually, they are people deeply blessed. In poetic, symbolic language, Proverbs speak often of the pleasure and joy of lovemaking. . . . "Let your fountain be blessed, and *rejoice* in the wife of your youth, a lovely hind, a graceful doe. Let her affection fill you at all times with *delight,* be infatuated always with her love" (5:18, 19 RSV). "My beloved put his hand to the latch, and my heart was *thrilled* within me" (Song of Solomon 5:4 RSV, italics mine).

Rejoice ... delight ... thrill ... words of pleasure and joy . . . words that put us in touch with ourselves as sexual beings and help to free us to enjoy our humanity *and* our spirituality. For part of our praise to God is in our emancipated celebration of sex, and in "guiltless gratitude" thanking him for his good gift.

9

A Love for All Seasons

I AM A "SOME DAY" jogger—some days I do, and some
days I don't. Today was one of my "do" days, and it felt
so good it almost convinced me I should jog every day
. . . but not quite. We have had an unusually mild and
lingering fall in Washington this year, the kind that
draws one out of doors and makes even jogging a joy.
However, one of these days the season will change
. . . we can count on that. Winter will arrive, and I will
be very content to jog through the upstairs hall, or even
in place by the side of our bed.

Yes, winter will come, and that is good. There is a
rhythm, a dependability, about the seasons that brings
a sense of well-being to me. Something in the cycle says,
"This is natural, this is right. This is as it should be." And
as it is with the seasons of a year, so it is with the seasons
of life—especially married life. Each season has its own
purpose, its own beauty, its dark days and its bright
days. Each season is meant to be lived fully, without
wishing for one that is past or reaching for one that lies
ahead.

Recently I was talking to someone who was research-
ing an article on women. The interviewer asked me,
"Aren't you sorry that you gave up all those early years?
First you were an actress, and now you are writing—
but in between there were so many lost years when all
you did was have a family."

Lost?

"No, I'm *not* sorry!" I said. "Those were great years,
and I wouldn't have missed them for anything. That
was a season in my life—one I enjoyed to the fullest."
I meant every word.

Married life does have its seasons. We change, and
the demands on our time and energies change. New
gifts emerge, familiar ones diminish. And this is all part
of the cycle, part of the good plan of God.

Being aware that there are seasons, and that one
season doesn't last forever, helps a person to live fully
in the *Now* of life. It helps a person to appreciate the
challenge and beauty of today. . . . At the same time it
provides patience for the difficult times.

For instance, in the season of early marriage, when
children are little and parents are up much of the night,
sometimes every night, for weeks or months, it helps to
know that this will not always be their life-style. So
during the years when the children need their parents'
physical presence, the parents can give themselves to
those demands without resistance, knowing that it will
end all too soon.

With four babies under the age of five, I was pretty

housebound for years. I remember my mother-in-law assuring me when she visited us that although "no one is more tired than a young mother, this, too, will pass." She was a great help to me . . . and when she told me that she used to fall asleep when she put her children to bed at night, I smiled—because the same thing was happening to me. But I could see that Mother had made it through those years and was, in fact, radiantly enjoying a new season in her life.

Yes, the early marriage years are full of hard work and production . . . the building of a career and a home. If the husband is the chief wage earner—and in most marriages, he still is (he usually is learning to specialize) —he may have to put aside some of his favorite pastimes and interests in order to develop those that are important to his work. Building a career consumes much of a man's time and energy at this time of life . . . but he also has a new life partner. And if a couple have children, they face the challenge of being parents . . . and these relationships deserve "prime time" as much as the career.

When children are young, a mother needs to give much of herself to them. But that doesn't mean she should leave her husband out of it all! It is the task of both parents to fill the emotional baskets of each child . . . to give each one the love, time, and commitment he or she needs to live life fully. Together, it is hoped, they will share life in a way so honest and real that it will earn them the right to share the riches of Christ with their children as they live life together.

Giving our children the commitment they need is good . . . orienting our total lives around them is not. There is a lack of health and wholeness in a totally child-oriented home. Dr. Alfred A. Nesser, of Emory University School of Medicine in Atlanta, Georgia, says: "Perhaps the most significant element in the dissolution of long-standing marriages is a consequence of living in the century of the child."

Children feel secure when they know their parents love each other. A couple's commitment to each other assures their children that they are part of a strong, loving, enduring relationship. And it is a relationship that frees, for as the children grow, they are not bound by it. When the home does not rotate solely around the children, the burden of the parents' happiness does not rest on their shoulders—nor does the home fall apart when the children leave. And so in this early season of marriage, a husband and wife should give their children all that is rightfully theirs—yet they must know that each comes first in the other's affections. "Mommy" and "Daddy" they may be to their children, but, one hopes, not to each other! Marriage begins with a man and a woman and ends the same way. A couple who are partners first, then parents, will not be neglecting their children . . . they will be nourishing them. They also will be building a strong basis for the seasons yet to come in their life together.

With such a heavy emphasis on production and work

in the early years, a marriage needs a little "theology of play" to balance the relationship. "The family that prays together stays together" is also true when you substitute "plays" for "prays." In fact, if it's all "pray" and no "play," there could be trouble ahead—the children are likely to bolt.

Some couples, because of their backgrounds, are naturals at play—others have to work at it until it becomes natural for them. Sometimes one member of the team is better at play than the other. In our marriage, Louie has the gift of play, and at one point many years ago I had to ask him to teach me. I had worked from the time I was twelve . . . at full-time summer jobs and part-time jobs during the school year. What I earned was not much, but my mother worked so hard to provide for us that the little I did earn was appreciated. That felt good, and somewhere along the line I became a bit of a "workaholic." Louie, on the other hand, had a more carefree childhood—not without responsibilities, but with lots of time and space for play. He also had a brother and two sisters close to his age—three marvelous people as well as ready-made playmates—whereas I was an only child. Ever since I have known my husband I have been fascinated with his stories of the family trips . . . the fun . . . the neighborhood boys and girls, and the mischief they got into together. Those early years served Louie well, for today if he has a free hour, he knows how to use it for fun . . . and he has literally taken me by the hand to show me the way.

When we were first married Louie took me backpacking into the High Sierra in California. Our packs
were homemade, our gear the simplest possible, but
what a good time we had! I wasn't "taught" to love the
high country—I "caught" it, and have had a strong case
of mountain fever ever since. Not that I don't like creature comforts when I'm down off the mountain and I've
been known to smuggle whatever creature comforts I
could squeeze into our packs—but the lack of them
cannot keep me from the high places. This is a gift I
would never have found on my own, a gift Louie
brought to our marriage and to our family life.

My husband also taught me to leave a stack of dishes
in the sink whenever the rest of the family was ready
to take off for a good time. How many times he had to
say, "Come on, Cokie, if we don't leave now, we'll miss
the beginning of the movie." The first few times he did
it, he almost had to pull me away from the sink, but
with practice it has become easier for me. Besides, I've
learned that if I insist on a perfect kitchen, I'll miss
more than the "beginning"—I'll miss the fun!

I'm surprised that so many people lack the capacity
for fun and leisure. Perhaps, like me, they need someone to care enough to teach them. Learning to play is
an investment, not only in the present, but in the future
as well.

When a friend called me recently to tell me, tear-
fully, that her youngest child had just gone off to college, I thought I understood. "Oh, Sally, you're sad," I

said, but before I could say another word, she inter-
rupted me with, "Sad? Who said anything about being
sad? I'm crying because I'm so happy!" Ah, yes, a new
season in her life was just beginning. Sally had been
happy as a mother with a very full nest (six children),
and now she was excited about stepping into a new
season—one that included a very interesting, creative
career for her.

Not all of us feel the way Sally does—some of us are
afraid—and I can understand. Being at home with a
family, demanding as it is, is like being in a comfortable,
warm nest. We are familiar with its needs, and from our
vantage point the world outside appears to be bristling
with responsibilities we feel we may not be able to
handle. And so some of us hold back, letting our gifts for
this season go undiscovered. Perhaps, because it gives
us a feeling of protection, we cling to a submissive role,
encouraging our husbands to assume responsibility for
our lives.

Protection? From what? From another of God's rich
seasons? We do not have to be afraid. We are created
to grow, to mature, to adapt.

Many of my friends—especially those who married
early—are going back to school. One woman is going to
school at night, taking one course at a time. Another is
going to the same university her son attends. . . . They
wave to each other in the halls. These women are not
resisting the middle years . . . they are excitedly preparing for them.

The middle years are full of potential. They are what

Ruell Howe calls "The Creative Years." They also are demanding years, as Robert Raines so poignantly describes them in his poem:

> Middle-agers are beautiful!
> > aren't we Lord?
>
> I feel for us
> > too radical for our parents
> > too reactionary for our kids
>
> > supposedly in the prime of life
> > > like prime rib
> > > everybody eating off me
> > > > devouring me
> > > nobody thanking me
> > > appreciating me
>
> > but still hanging in there
> > > communicating with my parents
> > > in touch with my kids
>
> > and getting more in touch
> > > with myself
> > and that's all good
>
> > > THANKS FOR MAKING IT GOOD,
> > and
> > > COULD YOU MAKE IT A LITTLE BETTER?

Someone has said that parents are people who give and give, and one day give away. It is in this middle

season that we give our children away. . . . They go off
to college, they find their place in the world, they
marry. For some parents the transition is easy, natural.
For others, it is a traumatic loss. When a husband and
wife find themselves alone in their home for the first
time in many years, that's a new season. If they have
kept their love alive, it will be a good one, for the real
quality of a relationship is determined by what is left
after the children are gone.

While a couple are still fully involved in these middle
years, it is good to begin to prepare for the following
season—the one that brings retirement and senior citi-
zenry.

We know a couple in their forties who have just
completed a university course called "Preparing for
Retirement." Experts in many fields—medical, economic, judicial, social, and spiritual—lectured and answered questions, and according to our friends, it was
a very lively course. However, as in every other area of
life, we can have all the knowledge in the world, and
it won't help a bit if our attitude is not right. When God
is active in our lives he helps us to develop the right
attitudes. He is the one who keeps us adaptable and
pliable . . . he is the one who urges us to swim with,
rather than against, life's forward flow.

Jung refers to us middle-agers as "the natural motors
of existence." If we haven't done it before, now is the
time to decelerate the motors just a bit and prepare for
the time when their productive powers will be stilled.

Now is the time to slow down enough to see people more clearly, establish deeper relationships, explore new opportunities to serve and to love. These are the things we can take with us into retirement and beyond. For love is the one thing that goes with us from this life into the next.

My mother-in-law often says to me, "Coke, you young people"—and by that she means us middle-agers—"ought to work on your dispositions, because when you are old, you will be just the same—only more so." How true! Charlie Brown's friend Lucy would agree: "The crabby little girls of today," she boasts, "are the crabby old women of tomorrow!"

When Mother Evans urges us to work on ourselves, she really means that we should let God work *in* us. He is our best therapist . . . he is the one who can straighten out the funny little kinks in our characters and smooth some of these wrinkles in our dispositions. If we are willing to change, he will do the rest.

Yes, the middle years are good years. They offer a couple the time they need to be together . . . the opportunity to let their children go and to enjoy them in a totally new relationship . . . to discover and use new gifts . . . and to grow in their inner life. We have found the middle years can be a renaissance of love.

And after that? I must admit, having not yet experienced this later season of married life, I feel at a disadvantage. . . . Certainly there is nothing I can say from my own knowledge. And yet, there are people I

know and love who are there right now. I have watched
—and I have listened—and because of what I have seen
and heard and felt from them, I am a believer in the
goodness of this season of marriage as much as any
other. Perhaps even more. For when a relationship between a man and wife has been a living, growing orga-
nism, will not the passing of seasons make it *more* so,
rather than less? Can the advertisement that says to a
woman, "You're not getting older. You're getting better," be true of a marriage as well? (Of course, we *are*
getting older—but you get the point!)

I think so! For I have seen the hands reach out—the
tender, knowing pats when they thought no one was
watching—the looks that belied the notion that beyond
a certain age people are "just too old to care about such
things."

And I have heard their words of affirmation for this
season of their life and love. My friend Helen Johns said
as she entered her seventieth year, "George and I have
never been happier. Life has never been so good." Seeing the look on her face and knowing the quality of life
they had together, I believed!

Of course, in this season, as in every other, there are
tears as well as happiness. . . . That is life. A couple
coming to the later years together walk daily with the
possibility of illness, death, and bereavement. One of
the dearest friends I'll ever have recently celebrated
her eightieth birthday. She and her husband are re-
markable people—in the way they live and the way

they are facing death. They believe that when they die they will leave a limited existence here and step into a whole new level of life with Christ. And yet they are honest about the hard times they are facing now. After the funeral of one of their best friends, my friend wrote me, "Now *we're* on the front line, and it's chilly out here."

Front lines are rarely comfortable, because that is where the action is . . . and in old age the action takes place in the mind and soul more than in the body. In *Learn to Grow Old* Paul Tournier says of this season of life:

> This limitation of life does not in the least imply resignation. All the renunciations demanded by old age are in the field of action, not in that of the heart and mind. They belong to the order of "doing," not that of "being." I live differently, but not less. Life is different, but it is still fully life—even fuller, if that were possible. My interest and participation in the world is not diminishing, but increasing.

How wonderful! This week I had the joy of hearing a speaker who is active in the Grey Panthers movement . . . and what a dynamo she is! When someone referred to her as a "young lady," she responded, "I am *not* a young lady. I'm an old woman, and proud of it!" Maggie has obviously learned that, like every other season, "winter" has its own unique joys of compensations.

Adaptability is a gift of the Spirit, and because that gift resides in each of us, we can meet the challenge of a new season. Our roles as husband and wife, our style and pace of life, will change over the years, but with God's help, each change will become a step toward a more thrilling future—a future in which we will be with Christ, and *all* those we love . . . forever.

But that is not all. For just as important as the number of years two people share—the chronological seasons—are the seasons of our feelings that determine the quality rather than the quantity of the years. For most couples there are seasons of emotional stretching—a shifting of gears from the images two people have of one another to the discovery of the real persons beneath the image. Hopefully, this is a time for the myth of perfection that inhibits many a marriage from being dealt with and seen for what it is—unrealistic and less than God's best. We might also hope for it to be a "season of the real"—real love for the real person you married, with all his or her strengths, weaknesses, and potential wrapped up in one beautiful—but very *human*—being.

How vulnerable we are to each other at this moment of truth in our life together! Will we be able to accept the real person we married? Or perhaps the question is: "Will I be able to believe his [or her] acceptance of the real me?" Someone has said that the ultimate in faith is accepting acceptance—whether from God or our partner. The moment we believe and accept another's acceptance of us—just as we are—our life begins to be different and can never be the same again.

In marriage it is this kind of acceptance that enables a husband and wife to walk through each season of life, saying to one another, "My lover, my friend. . . ."